REACHING
FOR THE
REINS

REACHING FOR THE REINS

Stories of At-Risk Students Empowered by Serving
Others through Equine Therapy

Tara Carlsen

iUniverse LLC
Bloomington

Reaching for the Reins
Stories of At-Risk Students Empowered by
Serving Others through Equine Therapy

iUniverse books may be ordered through booksellers or by contacting:

iUniverse
1663 Liberty Drive
Bloomington, IN 47403
www.iuniverse.com
1-800-Authors (1-800-288-4677)

Because of the dynamic nature of the Internet, any web addresses or links contained in this book may have changed since publication and may no longer be valid. The views expressed in this work are solely those of the author and do not necessarily reflect the views of the publisher, and the publisher hereby disclaims any responsibility for them.

Any people depicted in stock imagery provided by Thinkstock are models, and such images are being used for illustrative purposes only.

Certain stock imagery © Thinkstock.

ISBN: 978-1-4917-0727-2 (sc)
ISBN: 978-1-4917-0728-9 (hc)
ISBN: 978-1-4917-0729-6 (e)

Library of Congress Control Number: 2013916111

Printed in the United States of America.

iUniverse rev. date: 10/18/2013

For my students, with gratitude, for your honesty over the past six years. Your raw emotions and growth have warmed my heart. I admire your courage and willingness to be vulnerable in sharing your inspiring stories with others.

Contents

Foreword

I remember the day Tara Carlsen came to me with an idea. She was a young, idealistic teacher. This idea has blossomed into something extraordinary—a life-changing, service-learning program that has had an amazing impact on the lives of students with unique abilities and challenges.

I've known Tara for eight years. She is an excellent teacher and motivator of students. What I know now is that she is also an innovator—someone with passion to help our students become the best people they can be through service learning.

The book you are about to read will inspire you, motivate you, and move you to perhaps do something to be the one person that positively impacts someone's life. The students you will read about are real; I know them well. The stories are real, and the emotions that they evoke will stay with you. So be prepared to read about the importance of how our actions can help another person grow and what we can learn about ourselves through working with horses. This important book will prove that when we help others, we truly help ourselves.

Rich Klemm, director of nontraditional education
for Niles Community Schools

Preface

About two years ago, I started to take stock of what my students and I were accomplishing through the Reaching for the Reins program. I had just finished my master's degree in educational leadership at Ferris State University, and I was astounded that the educational world was not yet taking full advantage of what service learning had to offer students. As I looked back at the tremendous growth I had seen from my students, I knew it was time to share their success. After teaching in alternative education for eight years and running four extensive semester and yearlong service-learning programs, I can attest that students' personal growth through the process catapults them to a widened horizon of possibilities and goals as they graduate and move into life beyond high school. My goal in sharing these stories is to inspire you to implement service in your life, school, church, and community.

Acknowledgments

A special thanks to our volunteers, whose selfless dedication over the last six years has made the program the success it has been. To Cal and Sue for opening up their hearts and home to us; Aimee for her artistic eye; Jewel for all the little things; Gina for always making time for us; Kara and Dawn for having a big heart; Nanci for singing us a theme; Pat for recognizing our potential from the beginning; Joan and Ronda for their willingness to listen and make us laugh; Jennie, Hannah, and Autumn for sharing their horses; Wally and Christy for sharing their stories; and Cindy for her unique insight of horses. To all the others whom I have overlooked, thank you for your support.

To the numerous grant companies and a very dear friend, without whose generous contributions to the program these events would not have occurred and these stories could not have been told. Thanks to the Gateway Foundation, the Schalon Foundation, TEAM (Teens Exhibiting Able Minds) Foundation Youth Advisory Committee, Phoenix Fund, Heart of Cook, Flamingo Fund, local businesses, and individuals (anonymous). Your philanthropy has helped change our little corner of this world, one child and horse at a time.

To my incredible husband, Brendan, who humored my vision and spent countless hours editing and reediting and re-reediting, and whose literary creativity infused this endeavor with a life of its own. Your tireless dedication was the deciding factor in this book's creation.

Finally, I want to thank God for his endless and often subtle blessings. *Reaching for the Reins* is a true testament to answered prayer in my life. I have seen God's hand in many moments at the farm and have felt his direction in planning and securing funding. There have been many times where I was unsure of what to do next, and my answer was to surrender it to him, and he has on every occasion guided me through the next step.

Chapter 1

Reaching for the Reins

I believe every great teacher starts as a student who had a great teacher. In my experience I encountered two of these great teachers. I met Mr. D in seventh grade. Up to that point, I had come to recognize that school didn't come without a hard-won effort. Throughout my grade school years I struggled with academics. Mr. D showed me that I was capable of accomplishing anything to which I applied myself. He did not disguise that I would have to work harder than my peers, but he taught me that with motivation and hard work comes the joy of success. With this perspective, I applied myself with a tenacity that eventually led me to my second great teacher.

My introduction to Ms. K occurred toward the end of my bachelor's degree in an education methods class at Western Michigan University. Her approach to defining the boundaries of education blurred the lines between standardization and abstraction. Ms. K possessed a rare view of education that allowed her to see her teaching from the perspective of those most affected by it—her students. During one of her classes, she told a story that forever changed the way I solve problems as an educator.

One evening while cooking dinner, her year-old daughter began fussing as she played on the kitchen floor. Instead of becoming

1

frustrated with her, Ms. K got down on the floor and looked at the situation from her young daughter's eyes. She noticed that from her daughter's perspective, the only stimuli in the child's world were the drab cabinet doors and Mommy's feet scurrying about the room. Her solution was to remove a few of the cabinet doors and install a fish tank at floor height. As I transitioned from being a student to a teacher, I always told myself that I wanted to instill motivation in my students and use the fish tank philosophy for solving problems.

In August 2005, I married my high school sweetheart and started teaching mathematics at Cedar Lane Alternative High School less than a week later. My induction into the world of teaching was swift and clarifying. As I walked into class the first day, I was greeted by two of my students comparing ankle tether bracelets, each bragging about the distance they could travel without setting it off. This was my introduction both to education and alternative education. When I reflect back on this, I'm truly grateful for this context, as it provided a shock that I naturally associated with the term "alternative." The word means a million different things to a million different people. In the context of education, it might only mean five or six things to a million different people. It is with this understanding that I'll explain what my eight years of teaching these remarkable students has taught me about who alternative students are and what they're capable of when pulled back from the cracks they've been allowed to slip through.

Cedar Lane

Cedar Lane Alternative High School was established in 1990 as an alternative means for students who don't fit into the traditional high school to obtain their high school diplomas. Perhaps the most notable difference between alternative education and a traditional education is that alternative education attracts a broader spectrum of students whose difficulty assimilating into a general education format challenges their ability to obtain an equitable education. It is this quality that gives them a unique commonality with each other, an alternative perspective on how they might most effectively interact in their education.

Our students come from exceptionally diverse backgrounds. Some of the circumstances surrounding their journeys to Cedar Lane involve the death of a parent or parents, living in foster care, parental abandonment and complications from living with family members, health issues, rape, poverty, trouble with the law, and pregnancy and parenthood. For many of these students merely getting by from day to day is a struggle. Although all schools are comprised of students who come from these circumstances, Cedar Lane serves approximately ninety of the surrounding districts' hard-luck students who fall into at least one (and usually multiples) of these categories.

The vision of Cedar Lane is to help students earn their diploma and encourage them to integrate into their communities in a positive way. The school's mission statement is to ensure that every student

- succeeds academically;
- gains knowledge and skills needed to be a responsible, productive citizen; and
- appreciates one's self and others.

The Cedar Lane staff has worked extraordinarily hard over the years to not only meet state and national education requirements in unique ways that best serve the diverse student population but to also instill in the students a greater sense of community involvement and self-worth. Over the past eight years, the staff and students have revamped existing community outreach initiatives as well as having developed new ones. The Reaching for the Reins program was started in the 2007–08 school year to promote community service, and in the same year Cedar Lane spearheaded a Niles Gives Big donation drive that raised $70,000 in goods, services, and cash for a local family in need. These innovations turned the tables on what most people came to expect from an alternative high school. Instead of focusing on student inequalities, the school decided to embrace their challenges and, despite all odds, reach out to the community in big ways. Cedar Lane's and Niles Adult Education's accomplishments were recognized at the Michigan Association of Community and Adult Education award ceremony in 2008, where the school received the Program of the Year award for the state of Michigan. Yet even more rewarding than the award itself, the staff were able to announce that a record number of 2008 graduates were attending post-high-school training programs and college, more than at any previous time in the school's history.

With such success, one might think Cedar Lane is a state-of-the-art facility with the latest curriculum aids and cutting-edge technology. This could not be further from the truth. The Cedar Lane campus is comprised of a small brick building that served as the community elementry school in the 1960s. This building is called the main building and houses two classrooms, the facility's restrooms, and a computer lab/lunchroom, which is made up of hand-me-down computers from around the district. The rest of the campus is made up of four portable trailers, three of which are classrooms and the fourth of which is the office. Recently, grant monies were secured to update classroom technology to include Apple classroom projectors, and the district provided the school with four new student computers that are set up for students to create graphic arts projects.

Materital things and techology, though, are not what make an effective classroom. What makes Cedar Lane a success is people—

not just the dedicated staff who work together to ensure the best is offered each day to each student, but also the students themselves. Many of their backgrounds are inconceivable and most have been told or led to believe that they will not graduate and will never amount to anything in life. It is the courage and persistence of these students, each of whom decided to start over at Cedar Lane and use the opportunity to work hard to meet their goals, which make the school successful.

My Journey

When I started my teaching career, I did not understand my students as I do now. Like most people, I was excited to get a job right out of college and was eager and willing to learn. Over the course of my college education, I was indoctrinated with the knowledge that my first year of teaching would be crazy, but none of those warnings could have prepared me for the experience. There is an extremely high emotional and physical toll as you slog through your first real-world experience creating course outlines, developing lesson plans, conducting parent-teacher conferences, dealing with classroom management, and a whole array of other unanticipated firsts—all this while futilely trying as a new teacher to implement the multitude of strategies you spent five years of college learning about, only to discover their implementation in the real world is at times impossible, and is a far cry from the effective methods your textbooks boasted they would be.

It was not until my second year that I was finally able to "figure it out" and get beyond mere survival. For a teacher, this accomplishment brings a sense of ecstasy. This is, however, short-lived, as the real truth of the matter invariably dawns on you: you will never figure everything out, and it will never be smooth sailing. Teaching, despite its many eventual successes, is saddled with an equal number of failures and is frequently characterized by the struggle of coming to terms with many new and unique challenges on a daily basis. Yet, in my opinion, the expectation of new adventures lingering around the corner is precisely what keeps teaching meaningful and challenging and inspires the pursuit. I say *pursuit* because that is exactly how it feels to me—like I am chasing new concepts of how to engage my students to learn more and become active participants.

After two years I eventually settled into my role and began to gain an understanding of which methods were most effective in teaching math to a group of disengaged and rambunctious teens. It was only then that I realized math was only a small part of what my students needed. My obligation to them did not merely start and end each day in the classroom but extended well beyond that into a very real, very adult world they would soon be thrust into, ready or not. In them I recognized a need to learn responsibility, to have a place in a community, and to learn to work as a team, along with an array of other things I did not feel my math classroom could offer them. To this end, we started doing projects to tie the math they were learning back to real-world applications. But despite this, I knew they needed something more substantial, more outside the box. This is where I sat down on the kitchen floor and tried to come up with my own fish tank strategy for reaching these kids.

How Horses Came into Play

The evolution of Reaching for the Reins can very easily be traced back to a childhood fondness for horses. For about fifteen consecutive years, my family vacationed a week every summer at Camp Au Sable, a Christian family camp in Grayling, Michigan. My friend Sarah's family lived about four hours north of where I grew up in southwestern Michigan, and because we infrequently saw each other during the regular course of a year, our families vacationed together each summer. It was at camp where the two of us fell irrecoverably in love with horses. Most of the pictures of the two of us involved horses, cowboy boots, and cowboy hats, and our letters to each other throughout the year always included our hopes of new horse adventures. When I was in sixth grade, my family moved from the city into the country and bought two horses, one a fifteen-hand black-and-white appaloosa gelding named Shadow and the other a thirteen-hand buckskin pony named Nacho, who became my buddy. I fondly recall finding peace with Nacho throughout my own tumultuous teenage years, whether hanging out in the shed or taking him for a ride around our five-mile country block.

Nacho died my senior year of high school, and when I went to college, I simply did not have time for horses anymore, so my family eventually sold Shadow. Even though I no longer owned a horse, my horse-crazy nature never changed. Anytime I had a chance to ride with a friend or vacation somewhere where trail riding was possible, I jumped at the opportunity.

Introduction to Equine Therapy

While having lunch one afternoon with a friend, she casually mentioned her involvement in volunteering with the Therapeutic Equestrian Center (TEC), a local organization whose mission was to enhance the lives of people with special needs through horse-related activities. She told me how, one night each week, she volunteered at the farm, where she assisted a person with physical or cognitive disabilities with riding a horse. I have always been a person who seeks involvement and have enjoyed participating in church programs and outreach as well as school projects that promoted giving back to the community. While growing up, this involvement gave me a sense of community, purpose, and motivation I did not find elsewhere in my life. And since I am horse crazy, it occurred to me this might be the perfect opportunity for me to reinvolve myself in working with horses and satisfy a persistent itch for helping others at the same time. However, as the school year progressed, my schedule took me another direction, and my thoughts of volunteering went out the window. The school year ended, and I spent my summer working toward my master's degree.

My interest was rekindled the following fall when I saw a booth advertising for TEC at the local fair. I chatted with the volunteer running the booth and grabbed a flyer. As the school year got under way, I contemplated how I would work volunteering into my busy life. As my students trickled in and out of my class on that first day of school, I began to consider how they, too, would benefit from volunteering in their community at an organization like TEC and how much comfort I had received in my adolescent years from interaction with horses.

Our First Year

Determined to finally follow through, I pulled out the flyer, surveyed the website, and made a phone call to see if they would be interested in having a group of student volunteers. I got a warm reception from the director, who wanted me to stop by for a meeting to discuss how we could implement a program mutually beneficial for both their organization as well as one that met my students' needs.

As I pulled into the long driveway to the farm office, I could see horses grazing in a large pasture, and I began again to feel the sense of peace I remembered as a teen. The director and I retreated to a local coffee shop, where we could talk without disturbing the other four volunteers, who were bustling around the office busily keeping the nonprofit organization in motion. Little did I know the impact the decisions made in that meeting would have both in my life and in the lives of my current and future students.

We decided the program would start by bringing a group of students to the farm every other week throughout the fall and winter with the intent to learn how to work around the farm and to begin fostering a knowledge of horses. Then, in the spring, we would partner my students as teachers for a group of students with special needs. In order to stay in the program, my students would have to keep up their grades and attendance.

The next day at school, I pulled together a small group of girls and delegated them the honor of coining a name for our new program. They batted around numerous ideas, but it was our English teacher who prompted them to come up with Reaching for the Reins, which we often affectionately shorten to R4R.

The first week my students and I had no idea what to expect. We arrived at the farm eager-eyed and ready to work, uncertain as to exactly what we'd be doing. We stepped off the bus and were greeted by the young, enthusiastic barn manager, who took us on a tour of the facility and outlined our list of tasks to accomplish for the day. Quite frankly, I was surprised how hard the students worked. Though many had never experienced the manual nature of farmwork before, their collective enthusiasm made short work of moving hay, picking rocks from pastures, cleaning stalls, scrubbing bathrooms, and sweeping walkways. I was truly impressed at seeing what a dedicated group of teens can accomplish when given a little direction.

As the weeks progressed, the students began spending time learning the basics of horsemanship: how to groom and saddle, and the tricks for teaching someone to ride. The students learned to use a system where one student leads the horse and two others stand on either side to make sure the rider stays safe and secure in the saddle. I found it reaffirming to see their individual personalities develop as a result of spending time with the horses and each other. On more than one occasion, I observed students spending thirty minutes in a stall grooming, and when they emerged, it was evident they had gotten more out of the deal than the horse.

As spring approached, the director of TEC informed me a teacher had contacted her thinking their group would be a good match for my students to mentor as riders. Finding the right group of riding students was extremely important. We wanted a group of students that would benefit from the mentoring and horse therapy as well as show the Cedar Lane students their efforts were appreciated. We found this group with Lighthouse Education Center. Much like Cedar Lane, Lighthouse is a school for a population of students whose life journeys took them outside the traditional school setting.

Lighthouse

Lighthouse Education Center (LEC) is a center-based special education program for students that are severely emotionally impaired. The program is designed to help students from preschool through twelfth grade and supports about ninety students each year. Lighthouse meets students' needs by providing a structured setting to help in the development of skills such as responsibility, decision making, and acceptable social behavior. The program is focused on positive reinforcement of behavior. Students are very active in the process and review on a weekly basis their goals, decisions, and the consequences that come as a result of their behaviors. The ultimate goal of the program is to help students develop the skills necessary to reintegrate into their traditional education classrooms.

The population at Lighthouse is comprised of students from schools within the county, from which the most severe 3 percent of students who are emotionally impaired are accepted. Before a student is considered for the Lighthouse program, he or she must first undergo several interventions at the local school district, during which the student's behavior and progress are documented. If students continue to exhibit risky behavior such as shutting down, refusal to talk, persistent unhappiness, or explosiveness, they are recommended for transfer to Lighthouse.

Every student has an individualized education and behavior plan. These individualized plans provide students with attainable goals that allow them to demonstrate weekly progress, which helps students experience success and its positive benefits. Even though students have individual education plans, Lighthouse strives for schoolwide continuity between disciplinary and reward strategies, which help students transition from one grade to the next. To provide students with the safest and most structured learning environment, all staff members are trained in Cornell Therapeutic Crisis Intervention, which focuses on deescalating behavior but also teaches staff how to restrain students if they are being a physical danger to themselves or others.

In 2004, Lighthouse built a new facility that better accommodates the student-centered positive behavior support techniques. Each classroom has a special room in the back with a window to the classroom where students can receive one-on-one or small group instruction or that can be used as a quiet area for students to spend time working away from distractions. In addition to the secondary quiet room, the school has a supervised study room, where students who are exhibiting inappropriate behavior can spend some time away from the classroom until they are ready to take the necessary steps to reenter the classroom environment. A truly student-centered

11

program, Lighthouse also implements an after-school study hall program used to discourage students from making poor decisions.

Coupled with the disciplinary strategies, Lighthouse also employs a program called "Positive after School." Students can earn this privilege by maintaining a positive level of behavior during the school day. During "Positive after School," students stay after school and participate in activities such as cooking, physical group activities, and computer exploration. This incentive has a strong pull with students and compels them to work hard in order to earn this reward.

When Congress passed the Education for All Handicapped Children Act (EHA) in 1975, later modified to Individuals with Disabilities Education Act (IDEA), educational services for students with special needs began increasing significantly. Since 1975, schools nationwide are learning more about helping students with special needs and are rising to the challenge of ensuring that every student is given the best education possible. Lighthouse is an example of the teachers, administrators, and officials at the county level working together to provide at-risk students with a meaningful and positive education.

Becoming Mentors

The farm director, the Lighthouse teacher, and I thought these two groups of students would be a great fit for several reasons. First, each group had a social stigma in common. Both groups of students were negatively characterized because of their association with Cedar Lane and Lighthouse. We were hopeful this commonality would create a special bond between them. We were also optimistic their mutual social awkwardness would compel them to make allowances for each other's quirks. Secondly and probably the most important, both groups were looking for acceptance. The Cedar Lane students were desperate to be a part of something meaningful, and the Lighthouse students yearned to feel welcomed and valued.

Though extremely nervous about sharing what they had learned, my students' fears were quickly dispelled as the Lighthouse boys spilled out of their vans. Soon, everything fell into place, aided by a newfound confidence I had not previously seen in many of my students, who did an excellent job of instructing the boys on how to behave around the horses.

The first two years of the program taught my students how to work as a team, how to take pride in helping others, and how to be more personally driven. But even with this apparent success, I couldn't shake the notion that there was a way to make the program even better.

Circle "C" Stable

The third year brought several changes to our program. The previous spring the farm that had hosted the program the first two years closed, and the Therapeutic Equestrian Center moved to a new location. After a short period of searching for a new venue, I decided to continue the program at Circle "C" Stable. Cindy, the owner of the farm, had recently been introduced to Equine Assisted Learning (EAL) and was excited about the benefits my students would gain from being a part of these activities. She also had several acquaintances who were interested in volunteering their time to mentor my students.

In the fall of 2009, I accompanied twenty-five of my students on our new adventure at Circle "C" Stable. We were greeted our first week at the farm by Cindy and ten eager volunteers dedicated to helping them learn both about the farm and how to build positive relationships and make informed choices.

Equine Assisted Learning

Equine Assisted Learning is designed to use horse-related activities and the processing of those activities to promote educational growth and learning. EAL activities are conducted by a mental health professional along with a certified horse specialist and are designed around specific learning goals, such as teamwork, leadership, problem solving, and confidence building. A group of individuals is asked to observe horse behavior or complete a task with the horses. Afterward, the group discusses what they learned from the exercise. The emphasis is never on the completion of the task but instead on what was learned from trying something new. Horses are extremely intuitive animals whose instincts make them masters at discerning nonverbal communication. The horses' interaction (or lack thereof, in some cases) helps create situations that prompt discussions to help the participants realize new things about how they work as a team, communicate, and problem solve.

Volunteers

The volunteers who mentor my kids are some of the most caring and genuine people I have ever met, and it is their dedication along with the EAL activities that have helped raise the bar and turn what was a good program into a great program. Over the past three years, my students have had the opportunity to gain a deeper understanding of communication, relationships, trust, leadership, and responsibility, and to recognize the tools necessary for success and how to set and accomplish goals. The volunteers also helped them learn to tackle problems as a team, become more self-motivated, and have enabled them to experience the satisfaction that comes from helping others.

Benefits

Reaching for the Reins has not only helped the Cedar Lane students in their personal lives, but these transformations have carried over into their academic success as well. Students in R4R are required to maintain 80 percent attendance at school and pass five out of their six classes to stay in the program. This criterion provides them an extra incentive to work hard to get to school and perform well academically, which helps them toward their ultimate goal in high school: graduation. Over the past six years, students who have participated in the Reaching for the Reins program have passed an average of 20 percent more of their classes and have attended school 20 percent more than their peers.

Lighthouse students benefit from the program by having a safe environment to practice the decision-making, relationship, and communication skills they learn in the classroom. They look up to their Cedar Lane mentors, who do a great job of praising them for their accomplishments and teach them about trust and friendship and help strengthen their self-esteem. Since the horses interact differently based on human behavior, the students are able to practice body language communication as well as appropriate levels of energy and tone of voice. The acceptance and mentoring they receive from the Cedar Lane students, who are not much older than they are but whom they consider cool, has helped them grow in leaps and bounds, and their teachers have seen positive spikes in their school behavior in the days leading up to and following their participation in the program.

Memories

My memories of camp come to life when I read Sarah's letters and look through family photo albums, and I wanted my students to have something from the outset to remember their journeys with as well. Each week I hounded the students to pose for picture after monotonous picture, and on the return trip to school we would all take a few minutes to reflect on our experience through journals. The students' journals were sometimes guided by a prompt and other times were pulled from their own insights and range from a few random, disjointed thoughts to pages of well-thought-out feelings, memories, or lightbulb moments. The documentation from the pictures and journals have helped us all process and remember what we have learned from week to week, and have promoted a running dialogue between myself and the students as I respond to their writing, as well as having given me some of the details that made this book. In this book I have chosen to share the experiences of Reaching for the Reins with you through the students' stories. Many of the stories are followed by excerpts from student journals to help you see the program through their unedited perspectives.

Chapter 2

How Wisdom Saved Derek

Derek's Background

Derek slogged through school every day as disengaged as a student could be. He only spoke when prodded and never turned in an assignment. His disconnected behavior was exacerbated by his struggle to find transportation home from school. Day after day, entire afternoons were spent calling numerous friends and family members for a ride. All too often when he was unable to secure transportation, his frustration would compound into a level of anger unwarranted for the situation.

After two years of working with Derek, my colleagues and I had given up hope of ever seeing him graduate. We did not understand why he bothered showing up every day but never did any of his course work. With all our students, our primary responsibility is to build positive relationships and discover methods to encourage them to want to be successful, but with Derek our efforts appeared to be in vain. I recall on numerous occasions trying to engage him in conversation and receiving only a terse, one-word response for my efforts. He was a senior and was over three years behind his graduating class.

On a whim, I decided to encourage Derek to join Reaching for the Reins. I wasn't sure how long he would last in the program or, for that matter, whether he would even show an interest in joining because the requirements of the program are that students maintain 80 percent school attendance and pass five of their six classes. However, I reasoned that any involvement in the program, even if short-lived, would be good for him.

Convincing a reluctant kid to participate in something he or she has no cultivated interest in can, at its best, be an extraordinary challenge. Over the course of several weeks, stealing a minute or two where I could, I struggled to break through his monosyllabic stonewalling. Grasping at straws, I was hoping eventually to convince him he had nothing to lose in trying. I quickly learned convincing him was only the start. Over the course of a long month I prodded him to look at the paperwork, which, as the staff had seen from how he viewed his course work, could be an arduous and futile process. Finally, he unenthusiastically agreed to humor my persistence. When I handed him the eight-page packet questionnaire and liability paperwork, he looked at me as though I was crazy and gave it right back. Having gotten this far, I wasn't backing down. I smiled at him, asked him what he had to lose, and walked away.

Since Derek was eighteen and legally an adult, he was not required to take the paperwork home to his parents, and as I had never received an assignment from him, I was not optimistic he would return the packet. To my complete surprise, he did.

The Turning Point

The first week of a new Reaching for the Reins program is always full of anxiety and anticipation. Derek started his journey at the farm with a group of twenty of his peers. As the bus rolled into the

19

farm, the students darted uncertain looks from one pasture to the other, taking in the numerous duns, roans, paints, and bays, and the expanse of property and endless fencing, each of their eyes on a questing adventure.

We stepped off the bus to a warm fall day and a welcoming group of dedicated community volunteers. The volunteers embraced the group of reluctant yet curious students with warm smiles and a grand tour of the barns and paddocks. As the group made its way around the grounds, Derek lingered at the back of our herd with his head down and hands shoved deep into his pockets.

After the tour, the students were divided into two groups. Derek, along with nine of his classmates, was recruited to work repairing fences. As the group assembled fencing materials and screw guns and proceeded to walk to a far paddock to begin working, Derek remained on the fringes of the group.

One of the farm's most enthusiastic volunteers is Cal, a former construction manager turned farm maintenance hand. Cal is in charge of overseeing repair projects with the students. His specialty is a childlike spirit buoyed by a warm and understanding patience, the perfect person to teach the students about building and repair jobs around the farm. Every time Cal explains a job to the students, his goal is to engage each of them in a meaningful and positive way. Derek, typical to his nature, hung back from the group. Cal, sensitive to stragglers, determined to do something special to engage him. Cal admittedly has difficulty remembering names, so he employs a number of tricks to put faces and names together. Handing Derek a handful of screws, Cal read his nametag, on which Derek had scrawled Derek W. Seeing this, Cal commented that the W surely stood for Wisdom, and as the group proceeded to screw fencing brackets to wood posts, Derek began to melt.

The Power of Equine Assisted Learning

Self-absorbed teenagers rarely take the time to look beyond their personal drama at the larger picture of how they impact their world. The first Equine Assisted Learning (EAL) activity the students always participate in is designed to introduce them to the unique way horses communicate through body language and to encourage the students to consider their place in a team. Their participation in the activity is purely as observers whose job it is to note every detail of the activity and attempt to rationalize the horses' motives, movements, and moods.

For the first five minutes of the activity, the students observed three mares—Pink Maggie, Little Maggie and Moe—wandering around the dusty open arena. Pink Maggie and Moe, perhaps themselves uncertain about the students, stayed close to each other and the group of students, who were bumping the metal gate and making the latch clang. Little Maggie kept a discrete distance from the other two. Pink Maggie and Moe perked their ears, curious about the sounds the students were making with the gate and from scuffing their feet on the wooden observation platform. As the horses interacted with each other, they licked and chewed, a sign of horse contentment. As the minutes ticked by, Little Maggie sequestered herself on the opposite end of the arena. Slowly, she crept into the shadows as though no one would notice her disappearance.

Pat, one of the facilitators of the EAL activity, carried a handful of fragrant yellow hay to the center of the arena and dropped it unceremoniously on the ground. The three horses immediately flew into a flurry of action. Moe lowered her head and rotated her ears back and boldly walked toward the small morsel of hay. Pink Maggie, who was closest to the hay, quickly but cautiously scurried to grab a mouthful before retreating back to a safe distance to chew it. When Moe reached the pile, she began to devour it while keeping an eagle eye on the anticipated intrusion of her suddenly unwelcome companions. Little Maggie halfheartedly approached Moe and then Pink Maggie, but never while their ears were pinned back, and when they stomped, she retreated to the corner of the arena with her hindquarters to her companions. As the minutes ticked by, her head slowly began to droop.

When the horses finished eating, Cindy, the owner of the farm, supported by Pat, asked the students what they'd observed. As always with the first EAL activity discussion, the students were reluctant to answer and leaned back in their chairs with their arms crossed as if physically disengaged. Even when prompted, they tend to keep their answers short and without much depth or personal application, shifting their eyes back and forth to judge the reactions of their peers. At-risk students are quick to use the actions of their peers to help develop their own self-image, so, true to form, none of them wants to be the first to make himself or herself vulnerable through personal expression. Cindy and Pat, always ready for this initial reluctance, do a great job of guiding the conversation. As the group tentatively began to discuss what they had seen, Pink Maggie and Moe joined Cindy and Pat near the gate. Pink Maggie nudged Cindy for attention and visibly attempted to steal the show. Little Maggie, however, remained in her corner.

As the discussion finally took off, the students were given to understand that ear and hoof movement, along with head positioning, are nonverbal signals between the horses to establish dominance in a herd. The students recognized that while Moe and Pink Maggie were friends, the introduction of food induced Moe to assume a different posture, and the tone her body language projected became more aggressive. With this realization, they concluded that Moe was the dominant of the two and that horses do not have to talk or touch each other to understand what the other is saying. The discussion started to elicit a lot of important aspects about horse behavior and allowed them a little insight into what to look for when trying to interpret what horses are thinking and feeling. But even with these insights, Little Maggie's behavior remained a mystery. While the students could see what motivated the other two horses, they were unable to understand why Little Maggie was not interacting, and many interpreted her behavior as grumpy or mad.

Cindy used this opportunity to ask, "Do you ever see some of your fellow students off by themselves with their head down? When you witness this with people, what things could it mean?" This question prompted some of the students to acknowledge a certain pity for Little Maggie. They concluded that even though her behavior seemed to convey resentment or anger, it could be because she was not a part of the group and was prevented by the other two mares from getting any food. They reasoned that if this had happened over a long period of time it had the potential to make a person or a horse jaded.

The final question of this EAL activity is where students have the opportunity to apply what they have seen and learned to their own experience. When Cindy asks, "Which horse do you most identify with and why?" not surprisingly, most students, even though they appear confident in their interaction with their peers, identify with Little Maggie. There is something about being a teenager that inherently creates doubt and insecurity. Pressure from school, first jobs, dating, and encountering life-changing decisions turn whimsical adolescents into confused and awkward teens. The right of passage from childhood to adulthood is often a painful but necessary personal journey in developing the adult characteristics that make individuals more self-aware and self-reliant.

Baptism by Fire

Prior to Reaching for the Reins, most students have never touched a horse before, and Derek was no exception. The approach Cindy takes with the students' first interaction with the horses is baptism by fire. It's a great way for the students to learn to communicate with the horses using body language, and it helps to develop their teamwork and communication skills within their group.

While the horses milled around the arena, Cindy gave the students the simple instruction to bring her a horse. Because the halters are removed from the horses during this activity, the students have nothing with which to lead them. Confusion and uncertainty overwhelmed their faces as they broke into groups and hesitantly started toward one of the three horses. Most of the students gravitated to Pink Maggie and Moe. Throughout the day they were perceived as the most gregarious, and the students naturally assumed this translated into being the easiest to move.

Derek, followed by two of his classmates, headed toward Little Maggie, who was still standing against the far wall of the arena with her rump toward the middle of the arena and her ears pinned back. The boys timidly started to stroke her and encourage her to move, but she refused, and very soon Derek's classmates abandoned him in pursuit of a more willing subject. Derek was not so daunted. Out of the earshot of his peers, Derek continued petting her and started talking to her in a hushed whisper. For several minutes she simply stood unmoving, seemingly annoyed. Finally, she took a few tentative steps. While she was moving in the wrong direction around the arena, she moved, nonetheless, and Derek counted this a small victory. Seeing his progress, Derek's classmates rejoined his effort, but soon lost interest again after several minutes without further success.

After Derek's apparent failure to accomplish more than two steps, the reluctant pair was given little notice by the rest of the group. At this point the group had neither learned to work as a team nor how to communicate ideas with each other on how to encourage the horses to follow them, so their time was spent as islands of ideas with little cohesion in implementation. One student tried coaxing Moe with a stalk of leftover hay while another tried to herd Pink Maggie from behind with exaggerated motions, but their successes were limited to just a step or two from their equine partners, which eventually turned into disinterest and more milling about.

Unaware of the others' progress and oblivious to their varied tactics, Derek kept his eyes and attention on Little Maggie, goading her into taking a step or two at a time. By now his hand was simply resting gently on her back, his eyes down and his lips moving in private encouragement. Over the next ten minutes, Derek and Little Maggie slowly progressed around the arena to Cindy's side. It wasn't until then that he looked up with a smile on his face. Maggie, the grumpy outcast, was the only horse to make it to the instructor that day, with Wisdom by her side.

Derek's Fight

I would be lying if I said Derek never missed a day of school since and that he started turning in all of his work, but his involvement in the program was the personal catalyst for change that he needed. His work ethic suddenly changed, and he began to maintain the attendance and credit attainment required to continue participation. He began to interact more with his peers and no longer spent his afternoons fretting about rides; instead, he simply asked his fellow classmates, something he was too reserved to do before. Derek's battle is still being fought uphill, and his anger still emerges from time to time, but he is not letting it get in the way of accomplishing his goals. We all counted it a success when he graduated only a year behind his graduating class instead of the three he was originally behind when he started the Reaching for the Reins program.

It has amazed me these last five years how many lives the volunteers and horses in this program have changed. A simple nickname and an understanding horse set Derek on a different path than he may have otherwise found. I like to think Derek and Little Maggie found something in themselves they were able to reconcile with each other, some shared little secret between a boy and a horse. Winston Churchill once said, "There is something about the outside of a horse that is good for the inside of a man." I believe hope and encouragement can be found in any venue. Derek happened to find his in the kindred spirit of an outcast horse.

Chapter 3

Strength That Lies Deep

Most people see students who attend alternative schools as the "bad kids," but so often they are the kids who have struggled their whole lives merely to survive. They are strong, capable, confident individuals who need a place where they feel safe and accepted so that they can grow and learn to use their survival skills to better their future and, in many cases, the futures of those around them.

Mara's Past

Mara's father was murdered when she was two years old. Admittedly, she has no recollection of him. Mara grew up believing her mother's husband, a man who was both physically and emotionally abusive, was her father. Only when her mother divorced her stepfather when Mara was in middle school did she learn the story of her real father.

When Mara was two years old, her father sold a boat to a friend and, with the crisp new bills in his pocket, stopped by the local bar to celebrate his new financial situation. His wife at the time, having designs of her own for the money, hired a man to rough him up and take the cash. In the ensuing scuffle her father was knocked unconscious, and after waking to realize the money was gone, went to confront both his wife and the man who had robbed him. During this second confrontation he was stabbed in the back and died.

Mara's mother chose alcohol as her escape from her difficult circumstances. Following her divorce from Mara's stepfather, her mother bounced from one bad relationship to another, and Mara grew up caught in the middle. From this, Mara learned to hate the men who she saw as trying to fill the void she felt from having never known her real father.

When she turned thirteen, Mara moved from the small-town ghetto where she'd grown up to a small rural farming community, where she and her mother lived with her uncle. The move was positive in that she felt comfortable at the small school, but she found herself skipping more than she attended; and when at school, she was unmotivated to do her work. As a result, she fell behind on credits.

Just before the start of her sophomore year, she and her mother moved to Niles, a city considerably larger than anyplace she'd lived while growing up. When she saw the size of the school, she was overwhelmed, and without even attempting the high school, she applied to Cedar Lane the beginning of her sophomore year.

Moving Forward

Despite the continued struggles of her personal life, Mara was always positive and upbeat. She always tried to maintain a sense of fun and looked for every opportunity to make others laugh. She immediately fit in at Cedar Lane, taking to the small school atmosphere with ease, and she did a great job opening up and building relationships with the staff and students. And yet, her biggest struggle was making it to school every day and staying on top of her course work. She was doing much better than she had at her previous schools, but even with the increased effort she was not on track to graduate.

Mara's second year at Cedar Lane was the first year of the Reaching for the Reins program. Her class was part of the group of students that helped name the program. All of us flew by the seat of our pants those first few weeks at the farm. Even though we had a rough idea of how we wanted the program to function, there were inevitably some last-minute changes, and Mara and her friends in the program were always up for a new challenge.

Mara joined the program because she loves animals. Looking back on her childhood, she is unable to recall a time when she has not had a pet. As a child, Mara and her mother would get dogs from local shelters and take them home for the weekend to groom and socialize them in an effort to make them more adoptable. She has a soft spot in her heart for helping animals and humans alike, and being part of a program that did both fit perfectly with her spirit.

The first two years of the program were filled with a lot of work. Moving hay, cleaning stalls, and scrubbing bathrooms were a part of the weekly routine. Even when the work was tough, Mara and her friends pitched in and worked hard because she felt good being a part of an organization whose mission was to help others. On days when the group was tired, not feeling well, or it was extremely cold, she motivated her fellow students to make the most of the day.

Lifelong Memories

One of my favorite memories from those first years occurred on an autumn day when we were all out raking leaves. I became suspicious when a group of students adamantly encouraged me to join them in scooping a particular pile of leaves into the wheelbarrow. As I moved to skewer my pitchfork into the large mass of leaves, Mara roared out of the heap, flinging leaves everywhere. She and the other students laughed as I jumped away, and they talked about it for days afterward. For the next two years, she made it a point to constantly remind me of how she scared me that day.

While Mara seemed to effortlessly maintain a comical approach to life, working with the horses had a calming effect on her. No matter the drama occurring between her and her friends or in her life at home, it melted away when she was working with the horses. On occasion we would have spa days for the horses, where the students were able to spend several hours grooming and massaging the horses, and Mara begged to have more. She loved learning all she could and giving them all the companionship and love she was able to—one brush stroke at a time.

That first year I saw Mara become more involved in school and try harder in her classes. Oftentimes sports are used as a motivator for students to attend school and do better in their classes, but not all students are interested in sports. At Cedar Lane, motivation in these areas is also a part of the R4R program. It always amazes me how hard students work at school and on their attendance so they can go out and work harder to help others. Like Mara says, there is something about helping others that is addictive. It makes you feel good about yourself, and you want more of it.

Mara's Favorite Memory

The Reaching for the Reins program is funded entirely on grant donations from local grant companies, family foundations, and private individuals. Part of securing these funds occasionally requires me and a few students to present the program in front of grant committees. Toward the end of the first year of the program,

Mara and another student accompanied me to present in front of a grant company board. The following story is the story Mara shared with them.

Stanley was a sad kid who had some medical challenges that continually loomed over his head. He had a persistent scowl and refused to try new things. His group of mentors worked with him week after week, encouraging him to participate fully in the program, but he balked at every turn. The entire group of Reaching for the Reins students was aware of his struggles, and all began to view him as their collective project. It took several weeks before he agreed to groom a horse and another week to lead it. The goal was to get him in the saddle before the end of the program. It wasn't until late in the program that finally he agreed to ride. By this time the rest of the students from Lighthouse had been riding for weeks and were progressing into learning to trot.

When trotting was introduced, Stanley refused and insisted he was only comfortable at a walk, so while the rest of the students bounced around the arena, Stanley plodded along with his ever-present frown. The next week, however, the students finally convinced him to give it a try.

The whole group was focused on him as he turned the bend at the far end of the arena and approached the straightaway, where he would begin to trot. As the little pony picked up her pace, Stanley began to bump up and down in the saddle and miraculously his continual frown transformed into a smile. His teacher, who was standing at the side of the arena, wiped tears from her eyes as she declared she had not seen a genuine expression of joy on his face in months.

The talk on the bus ride home that day was of how the group had rallied around Stanley and how they all shared the joy of the day's events. Mara related the story to the grant committee with tears in her own eyes. The experience was a memory that touched her heart and showed her that helping others truly matters.

Senior Year

Mara's senior year brought more difficulty to her life. As the school year started, she ended a relationship and began a new one. As with any small school relationship, with a breakup and new relationships comes drama. High school years seem to always be marked with new and old relationships and the finding of oneself through the interaction with others, both as friends and more than friends. With the new relationships came new friendships, and when it came time for the R4R program to start in October, she and her new girlfriend and a small group of her new friends made sure they signed up. Mara was the driving force of the group. A couple of her friends were scared of the horses, but Mara assured them they would have fun.

Soon after the program started, Mara's mom went to jail, and Mara had to find another place to live. With her father's Social Security money, she rented a room from a friend's mom. This allowed her to catch the bus to school and maintain her attendance and grades so she could stay in the R4R program.

The Gazebo

Mara is a gentle spirit, and many of her happy memories from the farm bring tears to her eyes. One fall afternoon, Mara and her group of friends were assigned the task of painting the gazebo. As they worked they joked and laughed, and as any good painting party progresses, paint soon started to fly. Mara had her extra T-shirt wrapped around her head as a bandana, and her friends spread stain on the dried wood and each other. When they were done, they had greatly improved the look of the gazebo and diminished their own with brown splotches everywhere. Remembering the experience brings a smile to her face, both because of this experience and another.

The following spring the gazebo was selected for the unveiling of a carousel horse, Petey, the special rider's horse that would soon become part of the new Silver Beach carousel. Because he was commissioned to advocate horse-related programs and therapy, his sponsor thought it would be fitting to have him unveiled at the farm in front of all of the students. Mara had formed a special bond with Petey's namesake, a rescued pony that came to the farm the previous year. From the start, he loved his new job at the farm working with individuals with special needs. He seemed to intuitively know exactly how to cheer up those around him. Unfortunately, Petey foundered a few months after his rescue and was in so much pain he had to be put to sleep. His passing was extremely emotional for Mara, and she often visited his graveside at the farm.

Mara was one of three students who were given the honor of pulling the cover off Petey. The curator of the carousel explained to the group all about Petey's history and how every part of his design had special meaning. The hearts on his breast collar stood for all the love that goes into working with horses and individuals with special needs; the redbud flowers on his neck were to remind everyone of the beautiful trees abundant on the farm, and the horse and rider depicted on his saddle blanket showed the joy that comes from working as a team and experiencing success. After the explanation, Mara and her classmates pulled back the cover to reveal a beautiful palomino horse with a white horsehair tail. The students surrounded the little horse in the center of the gazebo to admire his intricate hand-carved and painted features. Looking at the horse, tears welled in Mara's eyes from a sense of pride in her involvement in the program and from the memories of the little pony that spent his last few months giving back to others.

Sources of Strength

Mara credits part of her graduation from high school to Reaching for the Reins for providing her the motivation she needed when she could not find it in herself to come to school. The sense of accomplishment and personal satisfaction she received from helping others was what dragged her out of bed and convinced her to come to class. In previous years she really struggled with attendance, missing weeks at a time, but R4R helped break that habit and established a new norm and work ethic. As the program progressed, she also realized she was a lot stronger than she previously thought. Instead of quitting or giving up when things got tough, she dug in and learned to work harder. Overcoming challenges made her feel strong and confident in her abilities.

She also saw her social life change and grow. Instead of focusing on the small stuff and drama of life, she began to look at the bigger picture. By not sweating the small stuff, she learned to have a more positive outlook on life and its challenges. She learned to focus on others and, in the process, has found a whole new passion in life.

Future

After graduation, Mara enrolled in a local trade-school program, where she received her personal nutrition, fitness, and massage certification. She hopes to one day work for a chiropractor's office, but in the meantime has taken a job as an aide in a nursing home and has found her true passion. She loves helping the residents live their lives to the fullest. For her it's not just a nine-to-five job. Instead, it allows her to build relationships with her coworkers and the individuals who live at the facility, and oftentimes when one is struggling, she finds herself calling after-hours to check up on them. Mara has a soft place in her heart for the needs of other people and finds herself the happiest when she is helping others. For Mara, Cedar Lane was the place where she took the broken pieces of her past and fitted them together into a life that continues to give back.

Chapter 4

Shining Bright

Hanna never acted self-conscious about her scarring. She wore short-sleeved shirts and tank tops like any other teenage girl. A lesser personality would have been intimidated or shy about them, but not Hanna. She pursued life unconcerned and unaffected by the things about herself she was unable to change. This, in fact, was the only thing that set her apart from the typical teenager, the casual indifference of how others perceived her. Most teenagers in her situation would not likely possess her level of confidence and strength.

When Hanna was two years old, she was scalded by the contents of a Crock-Pot. While jumping from a chair, she steadied herself by grabbing onto the power cord of the pot. The entire contents of a roast and scalding water burned her neck, arms, and stomach. She received burns on over 90 percent of her body, and the doctors only gave her a 30 percent chance of survival. The first six months after her accident were crucial to her long-term health and well-being. She spent her first month at the St. Joseph Medical Center in the burn unit before being transferred to Shriners Children's Hospital for another five months. During this time she had dozens of reconstructive surgeries. Her parents rotated shifts to stay with her, each spending several weeks before being pulled back to the necessities of daily living, each time replacing the other. Hanna has no recollection of the time endured there, but the doctors, nurses, and staff were tremendously supportive of her family. They encouraged her parents to keep a journal of the experience to later share with Hanna and help her understand the strength and courage she possessed to carry her through the difficult ordeal.

Hanna explains her scars simply as a part of who she is. They do not bother her, and she does not think about them as making her different. Her approach to life is that it can be whatever you choose to make of it, and one's attitude can be severely inhibiting or infinitely enabling. Because the incident occurred at an age too young to develop a self-concept, she accepts it as all she has ever known and maintains an uncluttered approach to how others might see her. This acceptance didn't necessarily come without its own scarring, as the passage through childhood presents its own battles. She recalled when, in third or fourth grade, a boy teased her about her scars. Her younger brother, who at the time was in second grade, settled the affair by punching him. The memory for her is more amusing than disheartening or sad.

Most of her reconstructive surgery occurred before she was three years old, but as she grew, the doctors continued monitoring her and determined she would need additional surgeries her freshman and sophomore years of high school. Even though she was allowed to make up her course work while she was recovering, she was not permitted to make up any tests she missed. This resulted in her having to take failing grades, which made it difficult for her to pass many of her classes.

Hanna came to Cedar Lane the beginning of her junior year. Like many students who find themselves at Cedar Lane, she hated

37

school and was behind on credits. Rather than dropping out, she decided Cedar Lane might support her goal of graduation. Both her junior and senior years, while at Cedar Lane she participated in a school-to-work program where students who have jobs attend school for half the day and work the other half. Students in this program earn elective credits for the work experience. Hanna worked at a nursing home and was adamant about wanting to become a nurse. Because of her extensive experience as a patient, she developed a passion for helping others the way she had received help.

Reaching for the Reins started Hanna's senior year, and, always eager to experience the most life had to offer, she signed up for the program with her best friend Rachael. Fixated on her post-high school goal, she signed up for the program with the hope it would benefit her ambitions of becoming a nurse.

The first week at the farm she dove right in and did everything she could to help. There were stalls to clean, hay to move, rocks to be picked up, bathrooms to clean, and aisles to sweep. She worked as hard as she could, knowing this was a way she could fulfill her urge to help others.

In September of her senior year, Hanna had another reconstructive surgery on her arm. The skin around her right elbow had become too tight, and she needed grafts to enable her full range of motion. She underwent surgery at the Shriners Burn Center in Ohio and spent seven days recovering. At the end of her stay, the doctors removed her staples and sent her home with a rigid sling that kept her arm at a 90-degree angle for a week. For six months after the surgery, she wore a pressure sleeve to help the muscle re-form to the graft and underwent physical therapy to help the skin stretch so she could again fully extend her arm.

During this process, Hanna did her best to keep up with her schoolwork. Her mother and friends devotedly picked up and dropped off her work so she would not fall behind in her classes, and she eagerly anticipated returning to school. As soon as the doctors cleared her, she returned to the Reaching for the Reins program and again tackled every task with enthusiasm.

For many of the Cedar Lane students, the highlight of their experience with R4R is the first time they meet the students from Lighthouse. Each week up until this point they spend hours working around the farm and learning about the horses to prepare them to help someone else do the same. When all this hard work culminates into their first meeting, they are both nervous and excited about the next chapter in the program.

In keeping with this, Hanna's favorite memory was meeting Michael for the first time. It was a cool spring day, and all the students were still wearing jackets, gloves, and hats. The Cedar Lane students were divided into groups of two or three and assigned a student from Lighthouse. Hanna was paired with Rachael and Louise. The plan for the day was to play some group games and then groom, saddle, and ride the horses.

When the Lighthouse boys arrived, there was a flurry of activity. Each group was trying to find their student and introduce themselves, find out each other's interests, and discover whether they had anything in common. Once introductions were made, everyone assembled in the arena for games. Hanna's initial assessment was that Michael was both polite and hilarious.

The first game they played was where the members of the group had to hold hands and pass a hula hoop down the line from one end to the other and back again. This activity requires teamwork, communication, and touch, things with which many students with emotional impairment struggle. It was intriguing to see how quickly the two different groups of students warmed to each other. Within the Cedar Lane students, the nervous butterflies flew away, and the Lighthouse boys' apprehension about interacting with new people dissipated. The groups of students immediately grabbed hands and set to trying to beat the time of the group next to them.

Next, the students brought horses into stalls and began grooming them. One of the most fascinating experiences is to see someone groom a horse for the first time. Horses are extremely interactive and highly intuitive. Because they communicate nonverbally through body language, they are more attuned than most humans at interpreting the subtleties of mood and attitude.

As Michael and the girls began grooming Sonny, a large paint palomino, Hanna remembers how nervous Michael appeared. The girls explained to him how to move the currycomb across his coat to loosen up the dirt and how to brush it away in short, sweeping motions with the dandy brush. The more time he spent with Sonny, the more he began to relax and grow accustomed to the twelve-hundred-pound animal, who is always happiest with his head right next to yours.

After saddling and walking Sonny a lap around the arena to acclimate him, the time came for Michael to ride a horse for the first time. Hanna remembers how tightly he clutched the reins as he rigidly adjusted his seat in the saddle. The girls had to remind him several times to relax and move with the horse and loosen his hands on the reins. As they walked him several times around the arena, the girls constantly engaged him in conversation, and he eventfully settled into the saddle and allowed his fear slip away.

During the spring of 2008, Cedar Lane spearheaded a donation drive campaign called Niles Gives Big. The drive was a spin-off of Oprah Winfrey's nationwide Give Big donation drive. The goal was for the entire district to spend a week raising funds and donating services to a local single mother of three whose husband recently passed away, leaving the family in financial distress. The youngest child was a girl who had several serious medical conditions. When Hanna heard about the girl's medical issues, she contacted the people she knew from Shriners Children's Hospital and filed the paperwork for the girl to be accepted as a patient. While the acceptance process is generally time intensive, Hanna was able to convince the hospital to expedite the process, and they agreed to set up an appointment for the week following the donation drive. The culmination of the donation drive was held at the district's middle school. Community members and students from all schools throughout the district gathered to present the family with gifts. During the presentation, Hanna gave a teary address in front of several hundred people in which she told the family about her wonderful experience at Shriners Children's Hospital and presented the family with the acceptance paperwork.

Hanna used every opportunity throughout her time at Cedar Lane to show her courage, strength, and perseverance. She bore her scars with dignity and was an inspiration to others. Over the last five years I have seen many students benefit in life-changing ways due to their participation in the program. Many students receive more than they have given, but I believe Hanna gave as much as she received.

Hanna remembers her time at the farm as positive and loved being able to give back. It solidified in her mind her calling to help others. She is currently married, has two children, and is attending a local technical college, where she will soon achieve her lifelong goal of becoming a nurse, so she will be able to further her work in helping others.

Chapter 5

Love Will Never Fail

Imagine growing up without parents. Your mom decided, due to a lack of money, that the best situation for you would be to live with relatives. Your relatives have good intentions, and they rally around you, but no matter how hard they try they cannot provide you with the consistency and support of a parent. You are bounced around from one school to another and from one family member's home to the next. What educational gaps, social insecurities, feelings of rejection, or anxieties might that create in your life?

These are the challenges Greg had to overcome. From the time he was born until he turned three, he lived with his aunt and a cousin who was eight years his senior. He and his cousin formed a special bond, and he remembers how much responsibility she took on for him in those early years. But because of changing family circumstances, he moved in with his father's parents when he turned three. During the time he lived with his grandparents, his father also lived with them on and off, which allowed Greg to develop the suggestion of a relationship that never fully matured because his father was not stable enough to have Greg move in with him. Greg understood that his grandparents wanted the best for him and that they tried to provide him with a good life.

However, by the age of thirteen, like any child, he longed to experience what living with his mother would be like. Greg had a brother who was four years younger who had always lived with his mother, and Greg wanted to have a "normal" family-structured life, as he believed his brother had. It was with this hope that he decided to move in with his mother. However, because he had never lived with her before and because she was not prepared to understand the inherent complexities of a teenager, she was unaware of her role as an authoritative figure. Over the years, the relationship she built with Greg was based more on friendship than it was on parentage, and she lacked the ability to provide him with the structure and boundaries necessary to be an effective parent. As a result, when she tried to put her foot down, he rebelled against her authority.

Since things were not going well with his mother, he again moved in with his aunt at the age of fifteen and started the ninth grade. Due to financial difficulties, he changed schools three times that year and fell behind with his credits. This brought him to Cedar Lane his sophomore year, where he set a goal to catch up on his class work. Though he was able to stay in one place the entire year, he was often caught up in the theatrics of high school drama, which made it difficult to concentrate on his schoolwork.

The following year he attended Cedar Lane for just a few weeks in the fall when he moved back in with his mother. This again resulted in him changing schools, as she lived in another district. Since he was the only member of the household with a valid driver's license, he became the family chauffer. With the privilege of transportation and the misinterpretation of what the keys in his hand meant, he chose to cut school a lot more often than he should have and soon found he was again struggling to pass his classes.

By the start of his twelfth-grade year he'd made up his mind to get back on track and graduate. The only way to accomplish this was to find a stable environment, so he made the decision to move in with his cousin, who had nurtured him early on and who by now had started a family of her own. This move, however, meant giving up the newfound freedom his driver's license afforded him. It also meant he could ride the bus to Cedar Lane and avoid the temptation of leaving whenever he chose.

Greg's cousin's house was by no means peaceful, but it provided stability and the basic necessities of life. The lack of peace was due to the fact that both his cousin and her fiancé each has three children. His cousin's children live full-time at the house. His cousin's fiancé's children spent every other weekend at the house, so when her fiancé's kids were home, the house was overflowing with activity and noise. On these weekends Greg tried his best to avoid the chaos of home. His cousin's kids are about eight years younger than he, and he felt like helping her raise them was his way of returning the favor of the care and support he experienced from her as he was growing up. Even though his home life was busy and hectic at times, the transfer helped him tremendously. He focused more on his schooling and was once again on track to graduate.

Through the six different school changes during his high school experience, he encountered bullying, large class sizes, and unhelpful teachers. A student who transfers partway through a year usually finds it difficult to develop meaningful, lasting relationships. It is also a challenge to navigate the idiosyncrasies of a new school, figure out new class expectations, and deal with the educational differences in curriculum. For example, different schools may use different textbooks, which approach material in different ways, or they may cover material in a different sequence. At times following his numerous transfers, the material covered in his classes was either a review of something he'd already learned at his previous school or was something entirely new to him with which he should have already been familiar.

These experiences left him a bit socially insecure and taught him the vitality of self-reliance. He learned to expect the unexpected and to keep an additional set of goals in reserve. When his life turned upside down, he became good at reconfiguring his goals to meet his new circumstances. He grew to understand that his goals were what kept him focused and that he always needed to be working toward something.

Greg was a very different student his senior year at Cedar Lane from the one I had known just two years earlier. He set himself apart from his peers with his driven nature. He often approached my desk to inquire into whether he had any missing work. When I informed him that he was up to date on his work or that he easily had an A in the class, he would persist with the question. For Greg, a passing grade wasn't sufficient. He also wanted to have completed every assignment. Unlike many of the other students, a passing grade simply wasn't good enough.

Greg returned to Cedar Lane in October of his senior year just as I was starting to get my list of students together for that year's Reaching for the Reins program. Every year I have about twice as many students apply for the program as there are slots available. Each year before the program kicks off, I hold a meeting about the program in which I require the students to fill out a lengthy questionnaire to gauge their interest. Greg had not yet transferred into school when I held the meeting and, therefore, had not had a chance to fill out the questionnaire. As soon as I became aware of his transfer, I added him to the list for the current year, suspecting he'd be interested. Greg had been in R4R his tenth-grade year, and since he'd done such a great job his first year in R4R, I thought his involvement would be a positive example for his peers this time around. The first thing he asked me several days later when he arrived was whether he'd enrolled in school early enough to be able to participate in R4R. When I told him I saved him a slot, he said it felt like he'd "won the lottery."

Greg is a natural leader and teacher, with the ability to explain material in meticulous detail without condescension or belittling a learner's intelligence. He so patiently explains and reexplains processes and is truly proud of his students when they accomplish the goals he has set out for them to achieve. One of the ways we prepare Cedar Lane students for teaching Lighthouse students is to have the volunteers pretend they are fifth-, sixth- and seventh-grade students without any horse experience. The volunteers love their roles and have a tendency to be very difficult and disobedient students. While practicing with the volunteers, who particularly enjoy giving the Cedar Lane students a hard time, Greg plays his part and truly takes the time to learn how to be a patient, gentle teacher in any difficult situation.

One of Greg's shining moments was his senior year when the Lighthouse boys first came to the farm. Greg was intentionally paired with our most challenging Lighthouse student that year, a kid who liked to portray an image of cool disconnectedness but who often made bad choices and did dangerous or inappropriate things.

The barn was crowded as the fourteen Cedar Lane students and seven Lighthouse students milled around the wide concrete aisle trying to find their partners. Mrs. Olson and I were facilitating student groupings and watched as Greg and Kevin met for the first time, shaking hands before Greg immediately took charge. He escorted Kevin to the tack room to outfit him with a helmet and grooming brushes. Then he introduced Kevin to Ginger, a fourteen-hand bay with a white blaze and snip on her face and two white socks. Greg explained to Kevin that Ginger was a sweet horse but got nervous when a lot of people were in her stall and did not like fast movement around her head. Even though Kevin said he already knew what he was doing, Greg redirected his overconfidence and continued explaining how and when to use a currycomb. Greg demonstrated for Kevin how the currycomb is used in small circles. Then he showed Kevin how to wipe off all the loose dirt and hair. As they moved their way down the horse's neck, across its back and belly, and back toward the rump, he explained that this method is the most effective way to remove the dirt and hair from a horse's back and that it prevented brushing dirt back on top of areas that had already been cleaned.

As they worked, Kevin boasted about getting suspended for bullying another student and about other disruptive things he had done in the classroom. Greg gently discouraged Kevin's behavior and explained that bullying was not acceptable and could really hurt the feelings of his classmates. He also tried to get Kevin to see the situation from the perspective of the bullied student.

As they saddled Ginger, Greg let Kevin do as much of the process as he could. They went together to get the saddle pad and saddle, and Greg let Kevin carry the saddle to give him ownership and pride in the task they were completing. Kevin was not tall enough to put the saddle on Ginger, so Greg put it in place and coached Kevin on fastening the girth around her belly.

Greg assisted Kevin in walking Ginger around the arena before they tightened her saddle. As they walked, he explained the importance of horse body language. By paying attention to the horse, it is easier to work with him or her as a partner, and both the horse and rider generally have a better experience. Even though the too-cool student claimed he knew how to mount, Greg talked him through the process, explaining how the horses can get sore backs if not properly mounted. As Kevin settled into the saddle, he began to brag about how many times he had ridden and how good he was at it. Instead of enabling Kevin's behavior, Greg simply complimented him on what he was doing well and encouraged him to do a few things differently in order to improve his riding.

As the afternoon drew to a close, Mrs. Olson pulled me aside and expressed how pleased she was about how the lesson between the boys had played out. She said she could not have asked for a better teacher than Greg to convey to her student how to approach new situations and to reiterate that learning is a continuous process. Even though she had been apprehensive about her students' participation in the program, she was now confident that through Greg's guidance Kevin would gain a tremendous amount from being at the farm.

Greg's declaration that it felt like he had "won the lottery" intrigued me, so I later asked him what it was about the farm that was so important to him. He responded that R4R just feels right for him. He says he sees some of the Lighthouse students around the community, and it gives him such a sense of accomplishment when they come up to him and tell him about what they remember about him from the farm. These interactions and the knowledge that he is doing something good for others give him an immense sense of accomplishment. He realizes that everyone has talents and that this is one of his; he believes that if you have the talent and power to do something, you are obligated to do it in order to make a positive difference in others' lives. He says it also makes him feel good to know the volunteers care about him and want him to come back each week.

One of the moments that helped him realize his gifts was during his tenth-grade year. It was the first week the Lighthouse boys were coming out, and he was not sure what to expect and was afraid he would mess up. All the students harbor this anxiety the first week. However, his positive experience with the Lighthouse boys helped him realized he was more than prepared for the challenge, and it made him feel good he was able to use his talents as a capable leader to help others.

* * *

I have seen such tremendous growth from Greg these past three years. He acknowledges having been involved in frivolous high school drama, but now he has matured into a man who realizes what is important and is driven toward his goals. He is not only a leader to his peers but also to the Lighthouse students. As a result of his experiences in R4R, he has learned to freely give back to others.

Pat, one of our volunteers, says that being a part of R4R has taught her there is an immeasurable amount of love in the world. Too often, people are not exposed to environments where it is socially acceptable to portray this love in healthy ways. However, within an environment like Reaching for the Reins it naturally flows between all its participants: horses, volunteers, and the Cedar Lane and Lighthouse students. There are people in the program who know how to love unconditionally, and there are those who are in need of that love. The beauty of the family atmosphere at the farm is that these roles often change from week to week. When one teammate is struggling, the others naturally rally around to help him or her through the trials. I am confident Greg does not consciously realize it, but I believe it is love that has drawn him in. He feels safe at the farm and is able to express his love for others and his genuine ability to help others. There is not a week that he leaves the farm where he does not first take the time to give each and every one of the volunteers a hug. It's as if the boy without parents has found a dozen and a place to call home.

Journals

January 26, 2012

Prompt: Do you feel like you're ready for the Lighthouse students?
What do you think are your strengths in teaching others?

Yes, I am ready for the Light House Students to come. I feel
good about being responsible for them. It's great to know
that we make an impact on these children. I'm glad I can
be a leader and teach and show them how to do something.
Sometimes its ok to mess up, not everyone is perfect. That
is why we have Cindy or the rest of the volunteers to help
us on something we struggle with during the program. I
really do think I am a good leader and also a detailed teller.
I can explain how to do something in simpler terms for a
child to understand. Holy cow I can't wait until they come
to the farm.

February 9, 2012

Prompt: Do you feel like you're ready for the Lighthouse students?
What are you looking forward to in the program?

Yes I am ready for the Lighthouse Students I've been ready
this whole program feels natural like belonging here. Every
time I go to the farm I feel good about myself. I can't wait
til next time we go. How awesome is it going to be when
the students come? Really awesome I know. I've already
met their teacher Mrs. Olson. She is a very nice lady and
she's great with her students. I don't really know that I have
any weaknesses in this program. Maybe a thing I need to
work on is to be more confident in myself. Sometimes I
believe I have low self-esteem. I may not show it sometimes
but I do. Some things I do good are being a leader, great

communicator, and I try my hardest to make the situation fun. I am pretty sure I'm going to be A Okay.

March 1, 2012

What is something difficult that has happened to you in your life and how did you get through it?

One bad thing that happened in my life was not having a place to live. My mom, brother and me had to stay in our car for a couple nights. We just roughed through it. It got better. Everyone has bad times. You have to go through hell to get something good.

Chapter 6

Remember Your Courage

The Reaching for the Reins volunteers are the lifeblood of the program. They are there every week, in the trenches with the students, teaching them, sharing with them in joys and sorrows, and encouraging them through every situation. Every member of the team is special and integral to the program, and each has a different experience to share that teaches and encourages us to be better, stronger people.

Our lives rarely follow the path we originally intend. Some of us get frustrated when things are not going our way, and some embrace the change and take the opportunity to learn lessons from the experiences and, in turn, use the outcome to help others. The latter opportunity is the path Christy chose.

Christy started her career in her midtwenties, chasing her dreams in advertising and marketing. This led her to move to Chicago in her thirties, where she worked selling cable TV and radio advertisements. The job was demanding and cutthroat, and as time progressed, the lack of a positive work environment took its toll on Christy's conscience. This unhealthy work environment, coupled with the downturn in the economy, led her to seek employment as an office temp. From there she climbed the ladder to become an executive assistant for a corporate management consulting firm. The perks and benefits in her new job were terrific. Not only did she bring in a six-figure salary, but she also received free travel, discounts through many corporations, and substantial yearly bonuses. Despite having become successful, the corporate lifestyle was also beginning to take its toll on Christy's body.

As her life started to become busier and busier, she began to retreat with her friends to Michigan on weekends to embrace a slower, less hectic lifestyle. Several of her friends boarded horses in Michigan about an hour and a half from where they lived in Chicago, and she would join them to spend their weekends trail riding in solitude. In 2002, she purchased Hawk, a seven-year-old sixteen-hand quarter horse gelding only recently started under saddle. Spending relaxing weekends with Hawk was her new passion, and she began to long for a quieter life.

* * *

From a young age she had known she was not necessarily normal. Growing up in Detroit, she noticed in her late teens that she bruised easily. Several doctors' appointments later, she discovered her bone marrow was not producing enough platelets. But as a young woman with corporate dreams in her future, she never let the prognosis hold her down. In 2001, she was diagnosed with preleukemia. She ate healthy, routinely exercised, and lived every moment to the fullest. In the corporate world, the expectation is to participate in late-night meetings and business courting events. She often stayed out late and enjoyed social drinking in moderation. But as time passed she began to realize that this lifestyle tired her out more than it did her similar-aged colleagues, and the stress caused several bouts of Bell's palsy. She realized that eating healthy and exercising were no longer enough.

In 2007, needing a radical change, Christy used her yearly bonus to buy a house in southwest Michigan, where she took a job at Whirlpool as an executive assistant in the advertising department. While this meant a 30 percent pay cut and lesser benefits and perks, she was determined to slow her life down and maintain her health. The move put her closer to her family in Detroit and just a few short minutes from her beloved Hawk.

The change of pace, though, was not enough to change her medical conditions. Symptoms of fatigue, muscle aches, and headaches plagued her, and her blood counts continued to worsen. In early 2008, doctors conducted a battery of tests over the course of two months, finally diagnosing Christy with hypocellular myelodysplastic syndrome. Up until this point she had been living in denial that she was really sick, hedging her bets on a long-term health plan contingent on a healthier lifestyle. She had vehemently held on to the idea that her condition would improve and that she could avoid extreme medical attention. However, with this diagnosis came a hard truth: she had a form of cancer that would not simply go away on its own. She would need intensive treatment and a bone marrow transplant.

After researching three hospitals and the courses of treatment they recommended, Christy settled on Northwestern Hospital in Chicago, where her doctor recommended a bone marrow transplant as soon as possible because he was afraid her leukemia could transform into an advanced case if she was not treated immediately. His initial recommendation for treatment was two days of chemotherapy, a mini-bone-marrow transplant and a three- to four-week recovery time. The role of the chemo would be to knock out her immune system so that it would not fight her donor's bone marrow. The new stem cells from her donor's bone marrow would go to work repairing her red and white blood cell counts. With this course of treatment her chances of survival were 80 percent, and she was scheduled for the transplant in early May.

Christy was fortunate to have two of her four siblings who were bone marrow matches for her, and ultimately her brother was chosen as a better candidate. Decisions were made in early April, but preparations would take about a month, so her transplant was pushed to late May.

The extra time gave her even more time to think about her upcoming ordeal. Up until this point she had been busy with doctors' appointments and planning. Christy was vigilant about getting second opinions and doing extensive research, not only so she understood what she was going to go through but also to ensure that she was making beneficial and informed decisions. However, she was now faced with a waiting period, and as anyone would do, her mind started to obsess about things. Sometimes it's funny how our psyches choose what to focus on. For Christy, it was her hair. In her research, she found that she would not only lose all of her hair but that it would also probably not grow back for six months. The idea of what she would look like and the thought that she would have to live without hair for such a long time weighed heavily on her mind. In her oddly optimistic fashion, she concluded that obsessing over hair was better than worrying about other possible complications over which she had no control.

With her transplant only a week away, her doctor received a letter from the insurance company declining payment for the transplant. This would again undoubtedly delay her treatment while appeals were made and red tape was cut through. Again, Christy's mind was set racing. Her doctors told her that if she did not receive treatment soon her survival rate would be significantly reduced, but her insurance company refused to pay for the treatment. There was no doubt she needed treatment, only the matter of how far she and her family would have to go in order to pay for it. After a few weeks of fighting, the insurance company agreed to the treatment, and the transplant was rescheduled for mid-June.

The process finally commenced in early June with Christy's brother Tim donating his bone marrow, which was retested to ensure the match. A week later, Christy was admitted for her two days of chemotherapy. Finally, on June 20, she received her brother's healthy bone marrow cells. She shared the following excerpt from her journal entry that day:

> Well that went very smoothly! The techs brought up the frozen donor cells in a liquid nitrogen container. There they were, a small thin bag of red, reeling in smoke as the tech and nurse held it in their hands the Chaplain Peter duly blessed and I cried a little, it was so beautiful. When the cells came through the IV I could actually see them traveling through the clear tube and I said go little cells go! Now I'll be praying GROW little cells GROW!! Every day as the test is yet to come. All of my normal blood cell production ended as of yesterday's chemo, so I have about three days left of my own cells to go on. When they die, it will present my body with the opportunity to let Tim's cells grow in to replace those that were lost. So, starting Mon, Jun 23rd the real challenges begin. My strength is good and I've had only a few sour notes so far. Keep those prayers coming! I've got every bit of faith that whatever suffering I endure will be towards the betterment of my future life and the lives of those I touch.

Although the six-month ordeal leading up to her treatment seemed tenuous, her fight had just begun. Over the course of the next year

Christy experienced the highs and lows of her recovery. Six months passed before her counts were high enough that she could go back out to the barn and visit her beloved Hawk. But even as she was progressing, her platelets were not recovering as quickly as they should. One blood panel showed progress and the next showed regression.

Her most difficult struggle came the beginning of the following April. Almost nine months after her transplant, she developed pneumonia and found herself back in the stem cell unit at Northwestern Hospital. The pneumonia was caused by a virus that would not have made the average person sick, but for Christy's still weakened immune system, she developed all of the classic symptoms, both bronchial and gastro illnesses. Fortunately, modern medicine had developed Cidofovir, a medication that would help but that would be hard on her kidneys and immune system. Taking this medicine would require daily blood transfusions to try to keep her blood counts up.

As if this was not enough of a trial, Christy's insurance company again started to deny coverage. At this point, her options were to bankrupt her family to pay for her medical care or discontinue treatment. While Christy was sitting in the hospital weighing her options, she received an unexpected miracle in the form of a phone call from one of her dear friends in Chicago. He had heard she was back in the hospital with severe complications. Realizing that her insurance company may be giving her some trouble, he called offering to pay for her continuing treatment. Christy is a strong believer in God, but even this was more than she could have hoped for, and it gave her strength going forward in her fight.

As the days progressed, her lungs started to improve, but the infection had established itself in her bladder and kidneys and caused quite a bit of bleeding. There were days where she received five pints of blood in an attempt to maintain even her subpar blood counts. Even as her infection increased, she grasped onto the smallest amounts of hope she could find, continually determined to fight.

After two weeks in the hospital, with her kidneys continuing to lose blood, she broke down and wrote her wishes for Hawk's continued care if she lost her fight. This was Christy's lowest moment and one that is still painful for her to think about. After all she'd endured, this was the point she almost gave up. The ordeal confined her to the hospital for six weeks, and she credits her connection with her horse and her belief in God for having given her the strength to pull through.

In the weeks following her release from the hospital, she made it a point to visit Hawk almost every day. Her journey is not yet over, as she continues to deal with the side effects of her extreme treatment, but in true Christy fashion, she doesn't let it hold her back. Christy strives to be her own advocate and find treatments for the side effects while continuing to live a full life.

Christy is still the gregarious, outgoing person who twenty years ago started out her career adventure in Chicago. However, now she uses those talents in a very different way. Posttreatment, she still experiences a plethora of side effects that make the normally simple daily tasks next to impossible. Her fight is not yet over, but she balances the difference by giving back. The R4R program is among several blessed by her good days. Christy says she learned through her ordeal that people and time are precious and that she has a special talent for sympathizing with and showing compassion for people in difficult circumstances. Now she is using her time to work with local organizations to establish cancer treatment support groups, to help coach an equestrian team at a local community college, and to volunteer with Reaching for the Reins. She believes that serving others is her calling and that everyone should dedicate time to help reach people in need.

Christy shared her story with the students, because many of them live through difficult circumstances. She wanted them to understand that strength, hope, and courage can get you through much of what life throws at you. When difficulties insert themselves into our lives, blame is often the first line of retreat. Christy's experience is much like those of many of the students in R4R, and despite not having asked for it, she was able to use it as a tool to relate to them in a way many of us, fortunate to have been blessed with easier battles, are not able to do.

All of our volunteers bring with them a unique set of skills that, when brought to bear on community and fellowship, build a brighter promise of a better future for everyone they so generously help.

* * *

Nichole

> What I thought about Christy's story was that it was touching and sad. Almost made me cry. But thank God for her being strong and able to make it through all the horrible stuff she's been through. She's a very strong lady. I believe she did teach a life lesson that you're strong enough to do anything if you set your mind on it, believe in yourself and just push yourself. Not to take life for granted because you never know how short your life is. Make life the best you can and you get to where you want to go in life by being happy and positive. Her story will have a big impact in my life. I'm sure of it.

Ava

> Christy's story is good and powerful. Telling us how she almost died several times made me tear up. Most people take things for granted and don't appreciate what life gives them. Listening to her speak to us you could hear her start to want to cry and it made me think differently about how I view cancer.

Haley

> I think Christy's story was great. It helped re-open my eyes to realize that although I have gone through so many things in my life that were so traumatizing I also have things that are great like my family and friends.

Chapter 7

A Safe Place

From the first moment I saw Brandon I could tell the road he'd traveled to Cedar Lane was difficult. He was a nice kid, always clean and dressed fashionably, but his eyes told a story of hardship. He was timid and stuck to a very specific routine. In the mornings he would arrive at school and root himself to the bench right inside the door until class started. Then, as the hall filled with the milling chaos of adolescents, he made his way to class by melting into the shuffling crowd of students, making sure to be completely undetectable. During class he sat by, and kept to, himself. He struggled with his course work but would not ask for help or interact with his peers. His head was always down, his eyes darting back and forth over the rims of his glasses, his ears perked up, trying to pick up just enough social interaction to get him through the day while avoiding the notice of his peers. At lunch he didn't eat but instead resumed his lonely post on the bench.

Each morning as I walked into the main building, Brandon and I had the same exchange, as if rehearsing a script.

Good morning, Brandon!
It's not good, Mrs. Carlsen.
Okay. Morning, Brandon!
Yep, it's morning.

Brandon had a cloud of anger, fear, resentment, and intimidation hanging over him that held him back from doing all the normal teenage things. He interacted much better with the teachers than he did with the students, and he was resistant to trying anything new. It was clear to see that he was holding back and that he was unhappy. His actions and exchanges were just filler to patch the obligatory social niceties, merely a charade to carry him through the day.

A couple weeks into the school year, a few Cedar Lane students, of their own accord, decided to make Brandon their special project. Gus, a muscly farm boy, sat next to him in his computer class. Even though Gus never did his own work, he worked tirelessly to help Brandon when he got stuck. Because Brandon was rarely forthcoming about this, it required that Gus be his constant shadow, a role Gus apparently felt strongly about. For his part, Gus talked incessantly, which visibly drove Brandon crazy at times. Despite this, the corners of Brandon's mouth would occasionally turn up just a bit, and it was evident he relished the companionship, however unsolicited.

Never one to encourage others to settle for the status quo, Gus hounded Brandon to try new things. One day during health class, Gus and a group of other students were playing football while Brandon wandered the sidewalk nearby. When the football hit the ground near Brandon, he halfheartedly tossed it back. To Gus's amazement, Brandon's nonchalant throw resulted in a perfect spiral that hit its target without any noticeable effort. From that moment on, Gus had a new mission—he was going to get Brandon on the football team. Brandon turned him down time and time again, but Gus persisted, encouraging him to join whatever sport was being played.

Carie, another of our students, also started to pester Brandon about joining her group of friends before school and during lunch. She made it a point each day to find him on the bench and hound him to join her. True to his nature, Brandon refused time and time again, but she would not be deterred. Despite his aloofness, Brandon was slowly, unintentionally becoming one of the more popular Cedar Lane residents.

Brandon did not sign up for Reaching for the Reins of his own accord. Gus, Carie, and Mrs. East, the teacher's assistant who helped me with the program, aided me in pestering him into giving it a try. We talked the program up for weeks on end before he finally, reluctantly, decided to give it a shot, and then probably more to silence us than to take a chance.

* * *

The first few weeks at the farm are always full of new experiences and fast-paced learning. This can be overwhelming at first, but one of the main goals for all of the volunteers is to make the farm a safe place—a place where students who struggle at home or at school can come and feel at peace while they learn and grow; a place where students' backgrounds don't matter; a place where students who have been sick, bullied, experienced difficulty at home, been in trouble with the law—whatever the case may be—all start over with a clean slate.

Brandon fit into several of these categories. Not only did he struggle at school but at home as well. The previous year he'd attended a school of about sixteen hundred students. While there, he was inducted into the ranks of the bullied and struggled with his schoolwork. And like many students in his situation, no one seemed to notice. One awkward kid in a swell of sixteen hundred doesn't seem to catch anyone's attention.

His home life was little different. Brandon lived with his mom, who he seemed constantly at odds with, and his younger siblings took advantage of the drama between them. Quite often they were able to throw Brandon under the bus so that he and his mom fought even more. With no safe haven and near constant depression, Brandon became suicidal. His father eventually intervened and agreed to allow him to move in with him. This move provided a much-needed respite. The following fall he enrolled in Cedar Lane.

* * *

Brandon arrived at the farm with an undetectable self-worth, the effervescent Gus at his side. For the first few weeks Brandon participated in everything at the farm, but anytime there was a down moment he faded into the background with his arms folded across his chest. In the first few group pictures he always made his way to the back of the group, where he could disappear, his head barely visible from behind the crowd.

Over the course of the next several weeks, Brandon participated in repairing fences, farm projects to ready the barn for winter, and a lot of horse time. He learned to saddle and groom the horses and practiced how to teach these skills to others. Each week he worked with different members of the R4R group and volunteers.

Toward the end of November, Brandon started to change. Week after week, Brandon began to talk a bit more, and everyone seemed to notice. He still protested when we coaxed him to try new things, but after a few gentle nudges he'd give it a shot. What really came as a surprise was when he began to join his peers in the lunchroom before school and during lunch. And then, just like that, it was as if we had a new student. Before school started each day he would wander into my classroom and ask me questions about R4R or make small talk about what the day had in store.

Just before Thanksgiving break, Brandon explained in his journal the feelings and thoughts behind his metamorphosis. The students were assigned to write about something they were good at and something they needed to work on when working with their students.

> I'm good at listening and doing what my group tells me to do. I'm not so good at moving the horse so much but I try my hardest every week that comes. What's hard for me is every horse is different. They act so differently and every group is different that I work with. But every group I'm in is fun because every group is different. I like that. What we did today was hard but a little funny to see old men and women act like 5 year olds kids. But they are showing us how its going to be when the Lighthouse kids come but its going to be hard work. But I can take it. I am going to need some help with the stuff because I don't know much about what to do but I am going to do my best. I hope I won't get kicked out of the Reaching for the Reins its fun and I like it a lot and I love Cedar Lane also its so fun and easy. It feels like this is where I belong. I met some awesome people almost everyone is nice and the people are so fun in their own way. I think I found my place now.

I was so excited about all the positive change I saw Brandon going through. He was becoming a normal teenage kid. He even started teasing and picking on his peers in the spirit of fun. It was evident that he felt safe and comfortable in his environment, and he was growing by leaps and bounds.

* * *

The first week the Lighthouse boys joined the program was a huge step backward for Brandon. My heart broke as I watched him struggle that day. He was paired with two other Cedar Lane students and one Lighthouse student. The first task the group was given was to get the horse saddled and ready to ride. Brandon and his peers began the day by introducing themselves to their student. I paired Brandon with one of his peers who was a strong leader because I had hoped the example would help him integrate into his new role as a teacher. However, the new experience was extremely intimidating for him. He tried to speak up on several occasions, but with all the chaos of the new experience, his advice and teaching fell on deaf ears. Within just a few moments, he reverted to his former self and scooted out of the way with his arms crossed and his back jammed rigidly against the stall wall. As his group members worked with their student, he became an awkward onlooker.

I felt as if I failed Brandon that day. He had come so far, yet in one moment everything he had worked for and all the growth he had exhibited dissolved. The following week I decided to pair Brandon with another one of his peers who was a gentle leader. I explained to Phil that Brandon had struggled the previous week and asked that he keep an eye on him and encourage him if he struggled. Phil did a terrific job of helping Brandon integrate into the group and helped him assert his leadership skills with their student.

That week Brandon bounced back with resilience. Phil and Brandon's student was a talker, and he kept the conversation going and the mood light in their little group. The three boys worked great together, and I saw Brandon regain the ground he had lost. As the trio made their way around the ring, Brandon had a grin on his face, and I knew he had again found his safe place.

* * *

The last day at the farm that year was a flurry of activity. Students helped Cindy with a few spring-cleaning projects. I joined Brandon, who was wiping down stall bars. We talked about his plans for the summer and the following year. He hedged that he might not come back to Cedar Lane, and I assured him that if he tried to go to another school we would hunt him down and drag him back. He smiled, something he was becoming more accustomed to doing. Over and over that day he mentioned he might change schools, and all of his peers responded by saying that they would miss him. He was soaking up the attention, and it was evident he needed to hear he mattered to his friends.

For lunch we headed down the big hill to the already crackling fire to roast hotdogs. As the students milled around, gorging themselves on hotdogs, chips, and cake, the scene was bittersweet. This group of ragtag teens and volunteers was a family. I was worried that over the summer Brandon's path might take him through more struggles and trials that would cause him to lose ground yet again.

After lunch the group made their way to the barn to saddle up a few horses and go for one last ride. Brandon chose to ride Josie, a sixteen-hand paint. Josie is one of the students' favorite horses to work with due to her unnatural gentleness, a byproduct of her inherent laziness. For the first time, the students were going to ride with no help. Previously that year, when the students rode they were practicing for when the Lighthouse students rode, so someone always led the horse. But today they were taking the reins themselves. As Brandon sat on the horse, he reminded me so much of the awkward Brandon who had started his journey at Cedar Lane that fall. Josie was her usual unmotivated self, barely putting one foot in front of the other. If given half a chance, she would stop and look over her shoulder as if to say, "What are you going to do about it?" Brandon's response this time was much different than what I had seen from him in the past. The old Brandon would have shrunk back and enabled her laziness, allowing her to stand around and do as she pleased. However, instead of melting, he stood up to the challenge. He bumped her on her sides with his legs and gave her direct cues with the reins. She began to walk again but soon slowed and tried to stop. Before she had a chance, Brandon again gave her a few encouraging bumps with his legs, and she responded by plodding along. Even though the task was not easy, Brandon never gave up, and I knew he was ready for whatever life brought his way.

Brandon's growth that year warmed the hearts of the entire Cedar Lane staff as well as the Reaching for the Reins volunteers. Since participating in Reaching for the Reins, Brandon began participating in other Cedar Lane extracurricular activities. His story reminds me again how powerful simply having a safe place can be in someone's life.

Every year each of the students makes pages for the yearbook. They are able to customize their pages with whatever pictures and writing they choose. I remember the day he created his yearbook page. The predetermined layout of the page only had enough room for a short paragraph four or five sentences long, which was more than enough room to accommodate what most of the students wanted to say. I set Brandon to work and went on about my classroom tasks. After just a few minutes, he asked if I could help him create more room in the layout because he had more to say. We removed a few pictures and shrunk the text. However, in just a few more minutes he flagged me down again asking for more room. This went on two or three times, and he ended up with three-quarters of a page of writing. The program meant so much to him he wanted to share it with everyone in the group on his page. Brandon was conscientious about his writing skills, so he asked that I proof his work before publishing. To avoid drowning out Brandon's voice, minimal editing was performed. In Brandon's own words:

How I have changed …

Reaching for the Reins changed me. I used to be shy and quiet, but when I got to the program I started to be my self and I got to know my friends very well. I made lots of new friends. I'm glad I'm not the same person how I was early this year. I am shocked I'm still in the program but I'm glad I am in it still. I'm good at what I do so I hope I'm in it for my next two years. I'm so good at what do. I still don't get every thing but I can do it if I just trust myself. That's what I'm starting to do again. These past months it has been nothing but awesome. When I look at these pictures, I got to say this year went by so fast. Half of my friends got taken out, but at least I have my other half of my friends. A lot has changed when I join Reaching for the Reins. My whole life has changed. I became a different person. My family is proud of me and what I do in this program and my family is proud of me doing sports again. I'm good at what I do just need to get a little better at my game. I'm glad my friends help in the reins when I doing sport's or when I need help with something. I can always trust them no matter what but if I was still my old self I have not join the Reaching for the Reins. My whole life I wanted to change so this is my shot to change my life around. Joining Reaching for the Rein is a challenging almost every marking period almost half the teens get kick out of the group and make it hard and harder for the teens who are still in it but so far it's all good because me and Phil we help each other out from time to time. Our kid was all right he was good kid. The people who helps us before the Lighthouse kids came did a great job. It was a lot of work to learn all the stuff in a few months but we did it. I'm glad we did it because teaching the kid's is fun and easy. We are the boss to them kind of so I got to take care of the kid's. I remember riding horse at R4R it was easy because I ride a horse before so I knew what to do. But some of the horse had a bad day so I got watch the horse to see if they are okay or not or in a good mood. I'm glad I am in Reaching for the Reins so I can't wait for next year I would be so glad if I'm in it again but if not oh well I find away get back in it.

* * *

After spending the last session with the Lighthouse students, the students were prompted to write about their day and what they might encounter during the summer.

April 26, 2012

Today was really awesome mostly when we did the yearbooks. It felt like I was famous. Everyone wrote on my yearbook, It was funny when Evan signed his own yearbook. I think its awesome that my three best friends don't want me to leave Cedar Lane and come back next year. My best friends are Evan, Phil and Carie, but I'm glad I have them. I'm going to miss them, mostly Carie, she helped me so much. I don't know how I'd be today without her help. She is my best friend. This year is going by so fast. I don't know what I will do over the summer.

Chapter 8

Darkness to Light

When someone agrees to share his or her thoughts and feelings with you, it is one of the most special gifts the person can give. From the very beginning of their involvement in the program, the students are made aware that I will read and comment in their journals as well as type them up and share them with the volunteers. Knowing what the students are thinking and feeling helps everyone understand how to best facilitate their learning and growth through this process.

For the first few weeks of the program, the students' journals are fairly dry and factual. They generally revolve around the excitement of new experiences and horses they've taken a shine to. However, as the program progresses the students become more open with the process, exhibiting a greater willingness to share beyond a superficial level. They begin sharing what they're thinking, learning, and, perhaps the biggest breakthrough, what they're feeling. Some students only take a couple of weeks and others take most of a year. On a few occasions it has taken a couple of years to convince a student to open up. When they share personal things, it always seems as though they are bestowing something special on the reader, and it takes a hard-won trust to reach this point.

About halfway through the program each year I ask the students to write about something difficult that has happened to them. Most have never put into words some of their toughest experiences in life, instead bottling them up to avoid the unwelcome vulnerabilities that sharing brings. Sharing at this level never happens overnight, but when it does eventually occur, it serves to represent a coming to terms with *it*, whatever *it* might be; and when they reach this point, they understand this. So, as a means of respecting their right to share their vulnerabilities, they are always instructed to fold the pages of their journals over and write on them by name whoever has their permission to read it. Some of them will write that anyone may read them, while others might list a single name or two of individuals with whom they feel comfortable sharing. Still others prefer that no one share in these private experiences, including myself. The intent of the exercise is to encourage them to express themselves and their thoughts about the hardships in their lives. Sometimes the exercise only serves to have the students share with themselves the things up to that point they may have tried to forget. This by itself can be powerfully therapeutic. The following excerpt, used with permission, shows the depth of trust these students have by exposing the fragile skeletons of their vulnerability.

Samantha

> When I was fourteen I lived with my dad, he went out of town for the weekend and I asked him could I go and he told me no because he wouldn't be back until Monday night and he didn't want me missing school. I was scared to stay alone and my step mom and sister went with so I had to stay with my Aunt I barely knew. We played games and had fun all day until it was like 3 in the morning. I woke up to this guy I didn't even know over me telling me to come in the living room … I did. He started kissing and touching

me in places I didn't like. I didn't stop him because I was really scared. I didn't know him or what he was capable of. My aunt woke up and caught him so she ran him out of the house as I lay there still crying. My aunt called the cops and told me it was my time to call my dad. I was so scared of what he would say so I asked her to do it. My dad asked to put me on the phone and told me I liked what he did. It's my fault and that I wanted it to happen. Till this day I blame myself for it even though deep inside I know somehow its not my fault. My dad has me convinced. My mom was sad, but not as sad as I thought she'd be. It really doesn't bug me anymore because of how a lot of people acted ... I got used to being the bad one. I still wonder how my own dad/family could be so heartless. The only thing that got me through this situation is my sister Julie. She was the main one there for me. She would ask me how I was and be there for me when my world went crazy. I can honestly say that Julie is my best friend. She's the only person that gets me and doesn't call me names. My other brothers/sisters call me fat and ugly all the time. Julie has never said any bad things to me. I don't understand why I had to go through things. I do, but in a way I'm glad I don't because if not I would not be lucky enough to know what an amazing sister I have.

My heart breaks at times for these students, my children. Their lives are ravaged by tragedy and pain and their hopes calloused and hardened with scar tissue, and still they fight. This is one of the reasons Equine Assisted Learning (EAL) has been such a positive experience for them: it allows them to express themselves and work through their difficulties in a safe and nurturing environment.

Trust EAL

One of my favorite EAL activities encourages students to think about trust. Trust is such a difficult concept to understand and develop when you have never experienced it in a positive way. When the people who you are supposed to trust, such as parents, relatives, and friends, abandon you and abuse you physically, emotionally, and sexually, the concept of trust no longer makes sense. Instead, it becomes something that only an ignorant and weak person who has never lived through your world would think to do. For many of my students, trust is characterized as a deliberate and accepted weakness, something they can't afford to entertain to survive in their individual worlds.

The Activity

Students are asked to enter the arena, where several volunteers are holding horses. The students are asked to pair up with each other. Generally, the EAL activity facilitators—Cindy and Pat—organize the groups, but to start off this activity students are allowed to pick their partners, typically partnering with friends with whom they have built a relationship. Once paired, one student is asked to wear a blindfold. Usually the bolder of the two obliges, however reluctantly. Next, Cindy instructs the students that no one is allowed to talk, directing the unimpaired partner to take the blindfolded partner to a horse. It is always fascinating to see how the different students accomplish this task.

Watching the blindfolded students, some take bold steps, confident in their partner's responsibility, while the unimpaired partners almost have a difficult time keeping up. Others shuffle their feet inch by inch through the dirt, hands held out, groping wildly in front of them. Once they reach a horse, some students start petting

75

them and seem comforted by the contact with the animal. Others are visibly uncomfortable with the contact and step back.

Observing how the unimpaired student approaches the task of being a guide is intriguing as well. Some students stick one bony finger into their partner's back and prod them toward a horse. When they reach the horse, the guiding partner will step back and leave the blindfolded companion alone. Others will wrap one arm around their partner's waist and take hold of their arm, walking step by step with them. When they reach the horse, they may keep themselves positioned so that they are at the horse's hind end, shielding their partner from any danger of being kicked.

For the next part of the activity, Cindy asks the guides to move their student around to the other side of the horse. Some take their partners around the horse's head, the safer of the two ways to navigate around a horse. Others choose to take them behind the horse's rump. For an individual who is new to working with horses, walking behind a horse can be a bit nerve-racking because it is the most likely way to get kicked. Some of the guides take this into consideration and put themselves between the horse and their blindfolded partner to help their partner feel safe. Others push their blindfolded partner out in front of them, causing them to navigate behind the horse on their own and making them feel more vulnerable.

Next, Cindy asks the guides to take their partners to another horse and repeat the process. The students' comfort level around the horses and the familiarity between partners always affects how the students interact with each other. The pairing between two boys, two girls, or a coed group always affects the comfort level of how they touch and lead each other.

Once they have repeated the process, the students are asked to switch roles. Once the second student is blindfolded, usually the more cautious of the two, Cindy changes his or her partner and does not say who is guiding him or her. She then directs the students with the same instruction as before.

Again, the way the students interact is fascinating because, based on their experience the first time around, the new guides are often much better partners than their previous guides. If the blindfolded student was guided by someone who did not make him or her feel safe during the first round, he or she is often more attentive to the partner's feelings, staying closer and providing more physical reassurance than he or she was shown. Similarly, the guides who hid behind their charges begin second-guessing their own methods and projecting them onto their guides.

The Discussion

During the discussion afterward, students are asked how it felt to be blindfolded. Did they trust their partner to keep them safe? How did it feel to be the leader? Did they approach their role as a guide differently than their partner? Why did they lead their partners different ways? How did it feel to know who your partner was versus not knowing who your partner was? This is one of the EALs where I have seen the students open up the most, talking freely about what they felt and learned during the activity. Drawing on their individual backgrounds, they talk about the importance of trust in relationships and how trust is developed and broken.

Journals

Each of the students views trust from a different perspective. Some talk about what it is; others talk about what it is not, each student trying to define the characteristics of trust by providing some situational examples. Trust is a hard thing to put into words, and it rarely comes easy, even for someone who does not have difficult circumstances to overcome. It is crucial my students understand that trust can be a positive thing and that it plays a pivotal role in healthy relationships. Their journals give a glimpse into how they process trust and how it fits into the context of their lives.

Jason S

Trust is a crucial part of a relationship. A whole relationship is based on trust. If there is not trust the whole foundation of the relationship is gone. To trust is to put complete faith in someone or something. To gain my trust is not easy. I have to know you for a long time and to really trust you. I still don't trust some family members. It's not good to completely trust anyone.

Haley

It takes a lot for me to trust someone. I start with little things, like telling them things and see if they tell anyone. When someone gains my trust then they will always have it until they lose it. Then its way harder to earn that trust back. Trust is very important to me. It's a major quality I look for in friends and relationships. Because of what I've been through so much, I have to be able to trust my friends.

Sarah

Trust is important and if you can't trust anyone you won't have any friends. Trust is something you can show and feel.

I show trust all the time but sometimes it's hard even if you know that person.

Eric

To me trust is important in a relationship because I would rather have someone who would catch me instead of let me fall. Or someone who can keep my personal information without telling anyone. It takes honesty, maturity and caringness for me to trust someone.

Nichole

What it takes to trust someone is honesty & loyalty. It takes a lot for someone to earn my trust back after they've lost it. I'm sure it's the same with the horses and students trust is very important to me. If I don't trust you there's basically no relationship between us. Because relationships take trust.

Tory

For me to trust someone it doesn't take that much. All it takes is me to know that the person is caring for me and for them to show it. I usually trust people mostly after I met them until they give me a reason to not trust. Trust is important to me because it lets me know that someone cares about me and would do all that they could to keep me out of harms way and from getting hurt. Just like the activity that we did today with the horses and being blindfolded. We had to trust our partner and the horse. It was fun and I had a great experience.

Continued Growth

Equine Assisted Learning is an ongoing process that does not stop when the bus pulls away from the barn. The experiences and discussions are applicable to so many aspects of the students' lives and provide them a new relevance to real-world situations. The students' understanding of trust in their own lives will change and grow as they mature, and they will always have one more memory of positive ways to earn and cultivate trusting relationships.

Chapter 9

Moments along the Way

Sometimes moments in our lives are so powerful that they change our perceptions forever, leaving an imprint of unforgettable paradigm shifts. The most poignant ones can occur as easily as a "lightbulb moment," that unmistakable and sudden connectedness that allows us a glimpse into the window of other people's realities in a manner previously not experienced. The volunteers and I have had many of these experiences over the five years of the program. Sometimes they warm our hearts, and sometimes they break them, but each of us carries them because they bring us closer as a Reaching for the Reins family.

Joan Remembers Eric

Eric's birthday is in December, and it fell on the last day we would be attending Reaching for the Reins before Christmas break. He mentioned to several of the volunteers the previous week how excited he was that his birthday fell on the next date we were scheduled to attend the farm. During the thirty-minute drive to the farm, Eric was in good spirits. He wore a silly jester hat with eight colorful starfish-like protrusions popping out the top. It was a big hit with his classmates, and they passed it around, taking pictures of each other to pass the time.

The weather was Michigan-dreary, and tufts of brown grass bulged between patches of melting snow. When the weather turns cold, Cindy makes her basement available to the group to eat lunch in the warmth before braving the cold temperature for a few hours in the barn. Each week the volunteers take turns preparing food to share with each other and the students as a supplement to their school sack lunches. For many of the students, this socialization period is the most structured fellowship they'll have with anyone until the next time at the farm, and the time serves as an opportunity to recharge from the otherwise disorganized chaos of their daily lives. As the bus pulled up in front of the house, the students filed out and down into the basement to get warm.

Eric bounded down the stairs and joined his classmates, tearing into his sack lunch and the meatballs, fruit, and veggies the volunteers provided. When the group finished eating, I announced we had something special to take care of before we went to the barn. To celebrate Eric's birthday, one of the volunteers baked and decorated a cake. I led the group in a very off-key rendition of "Happy Birthday." Eric grinned the entire time we sang and declared as we finished, "This is the best birthday ever!"

Every year around Christmas, Joan remembers the joy in Eric's face and his genuine excitement in the experience. As she tells the story to others, she comments that the gestures made toward Eric were small—just a cake and a song—but they meant the world to him. She mused that if her children were only to get a cake and a song, they would question the lack of presents, as the gesture itself would not likely be enough. But for Eric, this was his rite of passage into acceptance. It was a moment that he realized he was important to others and that they cared for him. And that is all it took for both of them to find a lasting meaning in the moment.

Cindy Remembers Samantha and Lightning

Lightning is a character. The sixteen-hand chestnut gelding believes his purpose is to command the center of attention, and at twelve hundred pounds, he's not inconspicuous. In his quest to continually be in the mix, he tends to assert himself somewhat aggressively with his head. His actions are not a reflection of an aggressive personality but rather an attempt to insinuate himself into a role of prominence in whatever is ongoing at the moment. Because he can rarely weasel his entire body into position to make this happen, he usually just ventures in a bit too forcefully, using his head to push his way through. A comical character trait of Lightning is his constant need to be noticed. As unsuspecting barn-goers pass by his stall, he waits until they are right next to the door, and then he abruptly paws the door, making a very loud banging noise, which usually makes them jump. His intent is to get their attention and forcefully encourage them to give him a few moments of their time. On numerous occasions he has also been known to give people a hearty bump with his head while in the arena in the unlikely event they need to be reminded of his presence.

Lightning is great with the Equine Assisted Learning activities because he is extraordinarily intuitive and is an active participator. During the EAL activity on trust, he has been known to nudge an unsuspecting blindfolded participant, perhaps as a sign of reassurance or, more in line with his personality, to catch him or her off guard. No one really knows his intent, but he certainly fosters conversation, nonetheless.

Samantha, too, has a personality as big as life, and she and Lightning hit it off. In short order, the two of them appeared to perfectly understand each other's outgoing quirkiness. A couple of months into the program, Samantha received confirmation from her doctor she was pregnant. Learning of pregnancy is always a stressful time for a teenage girl. There are a million of what-ifs, social stigmas, and the pressure of telling family, friends, and teachers. Because of this, we try to keep students in Reaching for the Reins as long as we have a doctor's note that confirms their safety in continuing with the program. Typically, a few modifications have to be made to accommodate the student, and the biggest is with the horses. Cindy is particularly careful about which horses pregnant students are allowed to work with.

One afternoon Cindy was pondering which horse to have Samantha work with. She considered Lightning's connection with Samantha but determined he was too forceful with his head for them to be safely paired. As she surveyed the barn for a horse better suited to Samantha's new circumstances, she observed Samantha walk over to give Lightning a gentle scratch on the forehead. Lightning was tied in his stall with his door halfway open, allowing just enough room for the inquisitive equine to peek his head out while preventing him from flinging the door all the way open and scooting his hind end out, his favorite pastime. As Samantha reached her hand up to his forehead, Lightning lowered his head. Stretching out his neck, he gently rubbed his muzzle back and forth on her belly, letting a huge sigh of warm breath out his nostrils, as if reassuring her everything would be okay. As Cindy observed this, she concluded that there was no need to worry he would be a danger to her and that, if anything, she was probably safest with Lightning.

The power of horses is astounding. Cindy has never seen Lightning exhibit that level of gentleness before that day or since. It was as if he knew in that moment he had to step out of his normally boisterous character into a more nurturing one and give a young teen mom what reassurance he could to help her make it through the difficulties looming before her in the upcoming weeks and months.

Cindy Remembers Pallets

Reaching for the Reins is not just about horses. It is about preparing students for life in whatever ways we can. Life skills and teamwork are a huge part of this process. In addition to working with the horses, students participate in a plethora of chores, tasks, and projects around the farm. These activities teach them that through teamwork they can turn mundane jobs into something fun. And when they complete the tasks, they have a lasting reminder showing their talents and determination.

Some of the different tasks students participate in are cleaning stalls and water troughs. But also a concerted effort is made to find projects that teach them skills that will help them with repair or building projects in their personal lives. One such task Cindy and Cal devised was to build pallets for grain and hay in one of her smaller barns. This was a project that needed to be done for years, but one which no one had ever taken the time to do, so bags of grain and bales of hay continued to sit on the cold and damp dirt floor in the walkway of the barn.

After the students finished eating their lunch, Cindy explained to them that while one group participated in the EAL activity for the day, the other group would be building the much-needed pallets. Her hope was not only to get the grain off the dirt but also away from the wall, where mice threatened to chew holes in the bags. So as Cindy headed off with a group to the EAL activity, Cal took the second group to the small barn to start the building project.

After gathering boards, sawhorses, tape measures, and drills, the students set to work. Cal explained to the group how to measure out the lengths of the boards and use a square to make a straight line for him to use as a guide while cutting. Then he helped another small group of students measure an equal distance between two eight-foot four-by-fours on the ground. As Cal cut the boards, a group of students screwed them to the four-by-fours. All the students worked together as an assembly line team, and within forty-five minutes they had completed two eight-foot pallets.

Meanwhile, Cindy was in the barn conducting the blindfolded EAL activity. When the groups switched, the second group working with Cal moved the grain and hay, leveled out the dirt, installed the pallets, and piled them with grain and hay. Both groups were proud of what they had accomplished and excited about helping Cindy with a project she'd wanted to do for years but never had the time to do.

As things were wrapping up for the day, a giddy group of students gathered around Cindy and asked her to close her eyes so they could show her something. A student got on each side of her, each taking an arm, and led her to the small barn. With a dramatic flourish they told her to open her eyes.

Knowing what she'd find but caught up in the students' enthusiasm, she opened her eyes to the newly installed pallets and a cleaner, more organized barn. While her eyes took in the students' efforts, her heart observed much more. Were it not for the program, most of the students would have little cause to speak to each other, let alone work together, and many had come from backgrounds where teamwork is afforded no credibility. With this understanding, Cindy observed the true value of the collaboration from the afternoon's teamwork and the love displayed in the childlike innocence of the students' excitement of the presentation. She sensed the transformation occurring within them both individually and as a team. The presentation was an expression of their individual and collective appreciation for the opportunities she was helping them experience, and they succeeded in making it a special event that meant more to Cindy than perhaps any of them will ever understand.

Cal Remembers Greg

One of the things most important to me about Reaching for the Reins is that the personal growth and development each student experiences reach beyond the constraints of school and the program. I am elated with any positive growth any of us observe, but I desperately want them to use what they learn to accomplish bigger and better things with their lives and in their communities.

Late one Friday afternoon in early November, I received an e-mail from my director that the Board of Education had a slot open for the following Monday's board meeting. They requested a presentation on Reaching for the Reins. With the short notice I was a bit freaked, but I scrambled to find a couple of volunteers and a couple of my more reliable students and over the weekend cobbled together a video.

On Monday afternoon I sent Eric and Greg home with two missions to complete. One was to write up a three- or four-sentence speech about what they'd learned from being in the program. The second was to meet Cal, Cindy, and me at the administration building about a half hour before the board meeting was to start so we could do a quick dry run. As I knew they would, both boys showed up right on time. Eric brought his dad, and Greg was accompanied by his aunt. Both of the boys were nervous but well prepared, so our rehearsal went quickly.

As we stood around waiting for the meeting to start, Greg's aunt reflected to Cal about what a great kid Greg was and how she loved having him at Cedar Lane and in Reaching for the Reins.

She described how his behavior differed while at other schools than while at Cedar Lane and expressed that she knew he was in a good place and around good influences now because he was such a better person. She no longer had to fight with him about going to school, and his attitude since attending Cedar Lane had noticeably improved.

She was not the only one who noticed the change in mood and behavior. While many teens are not prone to any degree of introspection, Greg, too, was aware of the differences in how he felt and acted as a result of belonging to Cedar Lane and participating in Reaching for the Reins. As the meeting got under way, our group was introduced, and Greg and Eric joined me in front of the assembly. Cal, Cindy, and I briefly introduced Reaching for the Reins and showed the short video, a compilation of pictures and success data, set to the Reaching for the Reins song. When the video finished, the boys were up to speak. Eric briefly spoke about how the program had given him a newfound confidence and how it was setting him up for success and graduation. A self-assured Greg spoke about how it made him feel good to know he was helping others and that this feeling was spilling over into other aspects of his life. He stated how he loved knowing he could make a difference and that he wanted giving back to be a part of his life after Cedar Lane.

After the boys spoke, the board responded with several questions about what the boys and program were accomplishing. The next day at school Greg was all smiles, sharing with his classmates and teachers his experience from the night before.

I know when students leave Cedar Lane their transformations will have just started. It is my ardent wish that seeds of hope and determination are planted and that they will mature and grow in each of them over the course of their lifetimes, helping them develop into the best people they can be. I want them to be active agents of change in their own lives as well as in their communities.

During my interview with Cal, he recalled Greg's progress. He noted how evident it was that Greg recognized he had the ability to impact others in a positive way. This realization allowed Greg to begin making better personal choices that influenced his own life for the better. As time goes on, I hope that he never forgets the lessons he has learned and that he continues to use the roots of his experiences to build himself the strongest possible future.

Christy Remembers James

As time goes on, specific moments in the program that were poignant in their happening tend to fade. However, as a Reaching for the Reins family we are blessed to have the memories of numerous volunteers and students to help us remember and cherish the growth that has occurred and specific catalyst moments. When I interviewed Christy, she helped me recall the following memory. With its recollection, I was able to pinpoint the moment James adopted his new motto.

James lived under the assumption of "I can't." When he came to Cedar Lane, there were many things he believed he could not do. As he bought into our program—building relationships with students and teachers and becoming involved in the school atmosphere—his attitude started to change. All too frequently Cedar Lane does not work immediately for students. Many come there because they do not like school and, despite our attempt to make it more than merely a school, it is still by its virtue exactly that. Walking through our doors does not magically transform their education into a positive experience where they start coming to school every day, doing all their work, and staying out of trouble. Developing these behaviors is a process that starts with students buying into the ideology of the program itself—that the teachers at Cedar Lane are there to provide them opportunities like Reaching for the Reins to help them care about themselves.

James joined Cedar Lane during winter semester, and it took him until the following fall to truly settle in and buy into the program. Shortly thereafter he joined Reaching for the Reins. While signing up for the program, he made it perfectly clear he would participate in the program but was *never* going to ride a horse. Of course, riding is not a requirement, but despite many of the students' initial misgivings, all of them tend to gravitate toward it after being around the horses for a week or two. James, I concluded, was not likely to be exceptional in this regard.

James met his challenge one dreary afternoon late in the fall. That year the kids stopped asking what kind of weather they should prepare for and just prepared for the worst as, week after week, Thursdays were wet, rainy, and cold. On this particular day all the students were in the arena working three or four to a horse. For the activity, one student was the rider, one the leader, and one or two students walked on each side. The students took a rotation in each position to allow them all an equal opportunity to experience it from different perspectives. The concept has many benefits: the students learn how to lead, ride, and instruct the rider. They also learn how to peer check each other and work as a team.

In every group there is always a student eager to ride, and James naturally tried to make his six-foot-tall stocky frame shrink into the background when Cindy asked who would be the first one in the saddle. After several laps around the arena, she pulled his group into the middle and helped another rider up. After changing riders twice more, James could no longer pretend to be anonymous. He was up, and everyone knew it.

The standoff started when James's group pulled Dusty to the side of the arena, and Cindy brought the mounting block over. James firmly told her he would not be riding, and to make it clear there would be no negotiation, he crossed his arms in finality. James had taken the high ground. Cindy, undaunted and with a look of equally uncompromising tenacity, told him to get on the horse. Knowing he had been explicitly clear, he looked at her in disbelief as one accustomed to the final word, and there was a long pause. The air was practically crackling with tension. The other students, sensing the vague outline of a battle they had no stake in, faded silently into the background, keeping whatever encouragement they may have been considering quietly caged.

There comes a point when a moment of silence allowed to drag on too long, allowed to become a bulky, awkward thing, can tip the scales in either direction, often with a disappointing or counterproductive outcome. Perfectly anticipating this balance, Cindy repeated her previous statement in a stern but fair voice. James seemed dumbfounded that she would challenge him on the issue, especially since riding is not a requirement, and his confidence in the strength of his position started cracking at the edges. Cindy softened her third prompt. James, also understanding what hinged on his reaction and clearly surprised not to have won the standoff, slowly moved into action, climbed the stairs of the mounting block, and stepped into the saddle. He was timid in the saddle, and even though his student leader struggled a bit to make the horse obey, he stuck with his horse and his team for his obligatory laps around the arena.

The most amazing part of the story is not that he rode but what it has done to his confidence and attitude going forward. Since this episode I have yet to hear him say, "I can't." In fact, he even tells people now that he is a great rider. He also tells other students that if they join the program to not even attempt avoiding new things, because Cindy will make them try them anyway. From time to time he'll still admit he does not want to do his work, but he never says he can't do it.

One of the things that always makes me smile is when I see him helping his peers buy into the program. He motivates them through his new can-do attitude. On many occasions I have heard him tell his classmates they are lucky to be at Cedar Lane and that if he can do the work, they have no excuse not to.

Cindy Remembers Martin

Not all of the important moments happen at the farm. Cindy recalls a special moment when Martin, a Cedar Lane graduate who had been a part of Reaching for the Reins his senior year, looked her up at the local youth fair. Every year, Cindy tells the students she will be at the local fair each summer and invites them to drop by to see her and the horses. Not many of the students take her up on the offer, but the summer after graduation, Martin did.

Cindy was standing outside the arena watching one of her 4-H students perform. If you're looking for Cindy at any point during fair week, ringside is the best place to hunt her down. She takes great pride in watching her students showcase their year of hard work. Not surprisingly, this is exactly where Martin found her. He had with him his girlfriend and his son. Cindy remembers the pride in his voice as he introduced her to his little boy.

What surprised her most was how he no longer resembled the student she remembered from their first encounter almost a year earlier. She recalled the image of him as a new Reaching for the Reins recruit the previous fall—how during the EAL activities he often had his arms unconsciously crossed over his chest and how during the discussions his responses were crisp and guarded. Even though he stuck to his commitment to the program the entire year and did a great job with his student, he always seemed to be holding himself back.

Looking at him now, Cindy saw how he had transformed himself into a responsible young man who, having remembered his experiences with an apparent fondness, had taken the time to look her up, introduce her to those who were important to him, and show his family the horses with which he had worked. He was proud to share with her his recent achievements and what his plans for the future consisted of. His transformation from an uncertain kid into a confident adult impressed her, and she told him how proud she was of what he'd accomplished. For Cindy, it was rewarding for her to see that the memories, experiences, and relationships he'd formed at the farm stuck with him and that the growth he experienced continued to help him develop and mature even after he moved on with his life.

I Remember Lightning

Historically, the relationship between humans and horses has largely been defined by control. Following their domestication, horses were used for transportation and heavy labor. Oftentimes the load they were expected to bear was difficult, and they were kept in line by using whips and harsh bits. Even today, many of these techniques are still practiced. Cindy operates with a different model. As part of her instructional methodology, she focuses on building relationships of mutual trust and working with the horses rather than exerting control over them. A big part of her relationship building involves closely observing each horse, acknowledging its uniquely individual personality, and understanding how it reacts to external situations and behaviors.

Lightning is one of the horses we use often for EAL activities because of his extraordinarily intuitive and playful nature. The students quickly home in on his quirky, almost defiant nature and are frequently amused at his diligence in taking advantage of any situation. Lightning was a great horse for students who needed to be challenged, and Cindy frequently paired him with students to this end.

In 2010, following Christmas break, roughly at the halfway point in the program, the students returned to the farm full of energy and ready for their last practice session before taking on the challenge of their own students. Eager to greet their favorite horses, they surged through the barn like a wave. When they arrived at Lightning's stall, they came up short, and their uncertain expressions conveyed a depth of concern. Lightning was not exhibiting his characteristically playful antics. Instead, he was standing at the back of his stall with his rump to the door. Several of the students attempted to give him a reassuring pat, but he only raised his head slightly and looked over his shoulder, refusing to move or acknowledge their greeting.

A few minutes earlier, Cindy pulled me aside and informed me about Lightning, but she had not yet broken the news to the students. As they milled about waiting for Cindy, they discussed his behavior. When Cindy arrived a few minutes later, she explained to the students how, though he was only in his early twenties, he was developing problems with his feet and was experiencing symptoms similar to foundering. Foundering is when the lower leg bones shift in the hoof and cause lameness and a tremendous amount of pain. Foundering can be caused by stomach problems, subtle changes in diet, or overwork, just to name a few. The vet and farrier had both been out several times to diagnose his condition but were unable to pinpoint the exact nature of the problem. Lightning had rapidly declined over Christmas break, and the students were shocked by how sullen he'd become.

Over the course of the next few weeks the students constantly inquired about his condition, and Cindy tried different medications, diets, and specialized shoes to try to alleviate his pain and correct the bone movement. The students celebrated each of his little victories and empathized with his setbacks. Unfortunately, following several months of failed attempts to help him recover, Cindy made the decision to send him to another farm with a quieter atmosphere, where he could spend some time in the field to help his bones heal. Because his personality had been so vibrant, the students felt his sudden loss. Over the ensuing weeks, all of them inquired about his health and when he'd be healed enough to return.

About nine months after he left Circle "C," Lightning had recovered enough to where he was able to return, and it quickly became apparent the students weren't the only ones who had missed him. All the mares in the barn made it a point to greet his return, each stopping at his stall in transit to sniff noses. The following year, the students who were carryovers in the program arrived to the unexpected sight of Lightning. Watching their surprise and excitement in seeing him, as though seeing an old friend after a long absence, was reaffirming.

The students' intuition at the beginning of Lightning's illness surprised me. Quite frequently, teens are so self-absorbed they have difficulty sympathizing with and recognizing the needs of others. Because of his innate ability to inspire enthusiasm, they were able to build a special relationship with Lightning that allowed them to immediately intuit a problem. Cindy's teaching method encourages them to build relationships with the horses and each other and is immensely rewarding for them. Not only does it provide a benefit for them at the farm during the program, but it also trickles down to other aspects of their personal lives—how they interact with and regard other animals and people with whom they come into contact. The idea and practice of working together in all types of relationships and understanding each other will continue to be important throughout their lives both personally and professionally. Cindy knew that Lightning was not done fighting. About a year after his illness he started participating in EAL activities again, and six months later he was being worked under saddle for light lessons. He is not yet done with his mission of inspiring a new group of students each year and instilling in them a sense of community and service.

I Remember Being Surprised

When you put a tremendous amount of time and love into something, it refreshes the soul to know it is making a difference. On alumni day our fifth year of Reaching for the Reins, the kids surprised me. Alumni day is one of my favorite days every year. The students who finished the program in previous years are invited back out to the farm to reconnect with their experiences. It is reaffirming for the volunteers and me to catch up with each of them and learn about the varied successes they are achieving in their lives.

The first few minutes of alumni day are always magical. As soon as we arrive, there is a meet-and-greet frenzy of hellos and hugs. The friendships pick up right where they left off previous years.

The fifth year's alumni day was special because we had students from each of the years represented by at least one returning alumni. We started off with the traditional meet-and-greet, and then the Cedar Lane director, who joined us for the occasion, called for everyone's attention. Calling me to the front of the barn, he acknowledged my behind-the-scenes efforts in organizing five years of a successful program. Unbeknownst to me, three of the students had prepared speeches about what the program meant to them and how it had afforded them a new worldview. The genuine sincerity and heartfelt meaning expressed in their speeches struck a chord in me. Each of them spoke of how the program had personally touched him or her and how much he or she appreciated the effort required to keep it running. They then presented me with a custom Bryer Horse painted in near perfection to mirror my own horse, Rowdy.

The moment was special and very sweet, but what struck me the most was the forethought on the students' part that went into making it a special day for me. Several weeks prior to the event, the students decided they wanted to do something special to recognize my five-year dedication to the program. One of the students alighted on the idea of having a custom horse made as a scale model of mine, and he and Mrs. East organized its creation as well as the collection of donations to pay for the statue. Another student took a great deal of time to make a personalized card. The day of the event, the students called their own secret Reaching for the Reins meeting, where they discussed who would give the speeches and present the gifts. There was no shortage of them vying for the opportunity.

All these efforts behind the scenes showed me how mature they had become. Teenagers are not often good at remembering to show appreciation, so their gesture demonstrated a level of adult thinking I had not seen previously. For them to have come up with the gifts on their own and organize a structured meeting is a fantastic example of the positive impact a program such as Reaching for the Reins can have. The fact that they all came together in one accord and decided in an organized way how they were going to surprise me is unprecedented for people their age. Their efforts demonstrated exactly what the program was intended to inspire: a collective community with each other built on mutual trust and respect.

The level of pride I feel for everything they accomplish and the level of their personal growth is indescribable. It helps inspire me to continue fighting for them and spending the long hours it takes to keep the program running. I want them to know that the time they spent saying thank you has also touched and impacted my life. It reminded me that teaching students to learn through service to others is something that will stick with them their entire lives. Encouraging them to be involved in their communities in positive ways is a gift that will keep on serving everyone they come into contact with, and if we as a team can keep that perpetual gift going, many souls will be refreshed and have their lives enriched.

Chapter 10

Mending Fences

In a word, teenagers are difficult. Any parent of a teen will readily echo this sentiment as common knowledge rather than revelation. The fact remains, though, that the teenage years are a struggle, both for the teenager and the parent. At this volatile point in life, teens are beginning to experience making choices for themselves, which brings both the promise of freedom and the inevitability of consequence. Oftentimes, parents and teens disagree on the amount of freedom teens should have as well as the choices they make. This ushers a new tension, and often fighting, into the relationship.

Natalie and her mom were a classic example of this struggle. Disagreements about chores, curfew, friends, and grades strained their relationship to the point where they barely spoke. Both struggled to see the issues from the other's perspective.

Natalie came to Cedar Lane partway through her sophomore year trying to escape the drama of a larger high school and because she was struggling with her classes. She immediately connected with the smaller atmosphere at Cedar Lane and found that she worked much better with the more relaxed school environment where, to a certain extent, she was able to work more at her own pace.

Even though she joined Cedar Lane a few months into the year, we were still accepting a few students into Reaching for the Reins. Natalie signed up because she'd had experience both with horses and with people with special needs and thought it would be a fun way to earn an extra credit. Although she started a few weeks later than the rest of the group, she jumped right in with both feet and caught up with her peers quickly in terms of horse knowledge and farm experience.

One of the things that struck Natalie about Reaching for the Reins was the genuine generosity and thoughtfulness of the volunteers at the farm. Cal, his wife Sue, and Cindy take a vacation every year to Texas to visit Cal and Sue's daughter, who happens to be one of Cindy's good friends. While they were on vacation, I received an e-mail from Cindy asking for all of the names of the students in the program. While Cindy knew who each of them was, she wanted to make sure she had the correct spelling for each student's name.

The next week at the farm following their return from vacation, they called all the students together and presented them with bracelets with their names on them. Even the boys donned them with pride, and for weeks afterward they proudly sported their gifts.

The gift is not what stuck in Natalie's memory, but rather the fact that someone was constantly thinking of her, was proud of her, and wanted to encourage her. Cindy's gift showed her someone thought she was special and wanted to show her she was on their mind.

This small act propelled Natalie to strive to do the same for her Lighthouse student. When the Lighthouse boys joined the program that year, they too wanted bracelets, so Natalie and a couple of her friends set to making each boy their own reminder that someone cared for them.

* * *

Things were beginning to look up for Natalie, but her relationship with her mother was not getting any better. Natalie felt her mother thought she was taking the easy way out by transferring to Cedar Lane and wasn't giving her credit for her newfound accomplishments. Despite their ongoing feud, Natalie invited her mother to parent day the following spring.

One of the most exciting days at the farm each year is parent day. The students are excited to share with their parents everything they have learned and accomplished. Natalie's mother agreed to come, but Natalie was nervous about how the day would go.

The day was extremely busy. We combined our open house and parent day that year, so there were eager parents tagging along with their children as well as other community members, organizations, and donors who joined us for the day to see how the program works.

Natalie's mom tagged along proudly as Natalie showed her around the barn and introduced her to her favorite horse. The Lighthouse students arrived a bit late, and while the group of parents and community members was waiting, Natalie bravely volunteered to speak to the group about her experiences in the program. As she spoke, her mom sat proudly in the viewing area of the arena.

When the Lighthouse students arrived, Natalie introduced her mom to her student. After the introduction, she patiently oversaw him as he groomed and saddled Ginger, getting her ready to ride. With an obvious measure of pride, Natalie's mom watched her very grown-up and capable daughter take charge of the situation and guide her student through each step of the process.

On the bus ride home, Natalie's mom commented on what a good day they had had together. The experience at the farm had been good for both of them, and they both agreed that it would be an island in the sea of rough memories from this time in their relationship. That day, Natalie's mom expressed to her how proud she was of all that Natalie was accomplishing both at school and at the farm.

Those few positive moments at the farm have gone a long way in helping Natalie and her mother mend the fences of their relationship. Even though they have disagreements now and then, they have never let their relationship go back to what it was before parent day. Both discovered a newfound respect for each other and now are more willing to see things from each other's perspective. Even when Natalie moved in with her boyfriend, her mother was supportive. She called and texted her every day, determined to keep the lines of communication open.

Sometimes all it takes to repair a broken relationship is one good day, one experience where you come together and realize that the other person still loves and cares for you. Even though they were barely speaking, Natalie's mother agreed to come because she understood it to be important to her daughter. When she saw what a tremendous young woman her daughter was becoming, she was more willing to work with her during arguments. Natalie really needed to know her mom still cared for her, would be there for her, and would be proud of her. Natalie and her mom are looking forward to yet another parent day next year.

Journals

April 28, 2011

Today was really cool! I loved having my mom tag along. I got to finally show her what I've learned! She seemed like she had fun ... Me and my mom usually fight all the time but today was really fun. Just talking and not fighting.

Chapter 11

The Hero

The first priority for the staff at Cedar Lane the beginning of each school year is to build relationships with students. We have found this is often the first, most effective step in teaching students self-motivation. Here is how it works! If the teachers develop a positive rapport with the students early on, they are far more likely have a reason to do their schoolwork. The direct line of open communication helps them to feel comfortable talking with the teachers, and asking questions becomes second nature. Because many of our students come from backgrounds where questions are discouraged and answers are few, establishing and maintaining positive relationships is integral to our mutual success. As students begin experiencing the success that comes from performing their work, they develop a sense of self-satisfaction from their accomplishments. This develops the foundation for self-motivation—recognizing and being driven by individual achievement. While this concept isn't groundbreaking, the pressures of the profession impede many educators from actively taking the time to know each and every kid. While this feel-good approach prevents the teacher from immediately launching into his or her curriculum, I have found it makes the job easier in the long run. When a student is motivated, he or she does not require the individualized oversight required of disengaged students, which significantly minimizes the near constant reminders and follow-ups.

I can relax knowing they are comfortable asking questions when they are hung up. It is for this reason that we staff members try to spend the first few weeks in our classes interacting with students both in groups and one-on-one in the hope students will connect with and open up to us. This provides them more autonomy and allows them to interact with their education in a whole new way.

One of my favorite ways to empower students is by asking them to write a ridiculous or funny journal prompt for five or ten minutes. When they've finished, I take a few minutes to go around the room and have them tell me one-on-one what they wrote about and why. This shows them that what they write is important to me, and the silly stories help me put a face to a name and show the student we dour-faced educators do in fact have a sense of humor.

It was during one of these exercises that I met Eric. For a prompt, I asked the students to tell me about one of their pets. As I patrolled the room talking to students about dogs named Spot and cats named Fluffy, I recall wishing I had come up with a more interesting prompt for the day. Then I came to Eric. Eric was an unassuming, quiet kid who seemed content to go unnoticed—a normal kid if only somewhat shy in his new environment. Initially uncertain, he opened right up when I became excited about Jenkins, his pet goat. I told him that in the history of naming goats, there has probably never been a more apt goat name. And I now had a memorable story to put with a name and face. Eric and I had a good chat about his silly little goat, who I learned liked to box, and that night I told my husband about the clever little thinker I encountered that day.

A few days later our secretary, Mrs. Wolford, mentioned to the staff that she would like us to keep an eye out for her grandson's friend, who had been bullied at a previous school. She said he was really shy and thought it would take him a while to become accustomed to Cedar Lane. She suggested he might not be comfortable asking for help if he was struggling or if students were bothering him. I was surprised to learn this was Jenkins's Eric, who seemed like your average kid, hesitant but certainly not shy.

As the first few weeks of school progressed, our science teacher, Mr. Gardner, and I both noticed another student constantly hanging around Eric, which struck us as unusual, as they seemed an unlikely pair. Bullying is a refined art that assumes many abstract forms, and many students are professional artists schooled in the subtleties of this unfortunate craft. As we focused more attention on the new best friends, we quickly identified an unproductive element in their interactions. One day I saw Eric giving the other student, who was both older and larger, money.

When I pulled Eric aside and questioned him about what we'd observed, he confessed the other student had been threatening him for several weeks, and to prevent a more unpleasant interaction with the kid, Eric had been purchasing an uncomfortable peace. Eric went on to explain that he had been bullied at other schools and that staff members had done nothing to prevent it. Naturally, his previous experience translated into how he dealt with bullying at Cedar Lane, preferring his own methods to those in his experience proven ineffective. Like Eric, many students find it far easier to deal with the effects of bullying on their own, without involving an overburdened staff whose attention is divided a thousand different ways. This is a continuing challenge as a teacher, and building meaningful and positive relationships with students goes a long way in improving students' and educators' successes. Eric's bully was addressed in short order, and his safe environment returned.

By the time October rolled around—one of the busiest and most fun times of year for me—I began considering recruits to get another year of R4R under way. We had recently made the big shift in our program to Circle "C" Stable, and I needed to recruit twenty students to fill the program. Eric was at the top of my list. By this time I still didn't know much about him beyond the fact that he had some farm experience, that he had been bullied, and that he was struggling with making friends. I thought this would be a great opportunity for him to put his farm skills to the test and make new friends. I was excited when he jumped at the chance.

Since chronology can be the undoing of good storytelling, I will now jump ahead a month in my story to give you the full benefit of seeing how Eric's story plays out. By November, when parent-teacher conferences rolled around, we had been to the farm three times. Unfortunately, not many Cedar Lane parents show up to parent-teacher conferences, but I was delighted when Eric's parents appeared on my list. I wanted to share with them his progress and learn a bit more about him. Eric's parents are the type of parents a teacher loves to meet. When we sat down to discuss Eric's progress, Eric's mother couldn't have been more appreciative, and she expressed her genuine gratitude for what we had helped Eric accomplish so far that year. As parents, they were clearly pleased with Eric's experience in the program and shared Eric's journey to Cedar Lane with me.

Eric had attended school in another district for the previous several years. He was an A/B student up until sixth grade, when something started to change. Eric gradually became grumpier and introverted and stopped doing his homework, and his grades started to slip. By the time he reached ninth grade, he would come home from school and go straight up to his room, locking himself in for the night. He barely communicated with his family, and they were at a loss as to what they should do. They were aware he had been suffering from bullying, but even though they told his teachers and the school administrators about the problem, the situation was not handled. In December of that year, they decided to enroll him in counseling.

The bullying of Eric started in the sixth grade and had gotten progressively worse. It started as verbal insults once every few weeks, in which a small group of students would call him names or point out his differences or perceived weaknesses, but as the years progressed it became more and more frequent. By ninth grade it had culminated into near-torture, where he was bullied daily by groups of students whose escalating denigration wholly fractured his self-esteem and left him feeling powerless and without worth.

Eric began coping by reverting into a shell of depression and isolation. His depression increased to where he began entertaining suicide as a way out, and his counselor recommended in January that he finish the year in homeschool. Aware that homeschool might not be an effective long-term solution since he still had three years of high school to complete, his parents considered Cedar Lane as Eric's (and their) last hope.

Due to bullying and depression, Eric had learned to segregate himself in social situations and to limit his interactions largely to adults who, while not entirely reliable themselves in his experience, at least didn't make a point of picking on him. When he came to Cedar Lane, this was how he approached the world, and this is how we found him. This made it extremely difficult for Eric to make friends.

One of Eric's turning points came our second week of R4R in late October. The Michigan air was beginning to get crisp around the edges, and the students were beginning to bundle up. Eric was wearing a tan jacket over his favorite Notre Dame hoodie. After spending some time doing various chores around the farm, it was the turn of Eric's group to participate in an EAL activity. The students were challenged to complete a particularly difficult EAL activity where their task was to play billiards with two horses. The goal of this activity is to simultaneously get both of the horses in separate pockets on opposite ends of the arena created on the ground with poles. The students were disallowed from using halters or lead ropes and were instructed not to make physical contact with the horses.

As Eric and his fellow students milled around the horses trying to figure out what approach to take with the task, Eric hung back. As he'd had some experience with horses, he was not nervous around them, but was instead apprehensive about interaction with peers. The irony here is that Eric was far more concerned about being hurt emotionally than physically—that his couple-hundred-pound classmates were more intimidating than a twelve-hundred-pound horse. As Eric walked by Nate, a tall, handsome chestnut gelding, something remarkable happened—Nate stretched out his nose as if to discern whether Eric was worthy and then began to follow him. As Nate followed step after step behind Eric, the rest of Eric's classmates took notice. They began to rally around him and try to figure out how they could use Eric's magic to gain the cooperation of Moe, the second horse. Soon, Eric had Nate in one of the pockets, and the group began discussing how they could use Eric to get Moe in the other pocket. The problem was that Nate still wanted to follow Eric right out of the pocket he was supposed to be staying in. The students decided to crowd around Nate to encourage him to stay put while another group encouraged Eric to lure Moe. Several minutes later, Moe began plodding along behind Eric, and the group accomplished their goal shortly afterward.

During the discussion following the EAL activity, several of the students gave credit to Eric for being the central reason why they were able to accomplish their goal. Practically glowing from the praise of his peers, Eric was made to feel like he had singlehandedly accomplished what his peers were unable to collectively. Unbeknownst to either Eric or his peers at the moment of his success was that he was wearing his barn jacket that day, the same jacket he often wore out to the barn where he fed his goats. Afterward, when he pondered his success, he concluded it must have smelled like goat treats, because he was definitely a horse magnet. When asked how the EAL activity made him feel, Eric said he felt "like a hero."

From that day on, Eric started to interact more and more with his peers. In fact, if we return one month earlier to my parent-teacher conference, the rest of the story his mother shared with me was remarkable. The first part of her story shed light onto why he had been so introverted and leery of interaction with his peers. However, the second part of her story is a true reflection of how just a few simple moments can begin to erase the years of scars that once kept him so bottled up.

You see, Eric's mom told me that after he started attending Cedar Lane and, more pointedly, that after he started attending R4R, his behavior at home underwent a dramatic change. Instead of coming home each day and barricading himself in his room, he now interacted with his family. She even said that the previous weekend he had asked his dad if he would help him repaint his room and that they had had a great experience working together renovating what had previously been his cell of solitude.

Eric still has an uphill battle to fight. In full, Eric was with us for three years and, as of the writing of this book, has graduated. While he is still occasionally challenged from the difficulties of his life experiences, he is finding the tools he'll need to be successful in accomplishing his goals. One of those tools—a silly old barn coat—serves as a great analogy for what I'm confident he'll be able to accomplish with the rest of his life. Because of his continued successes, he is becoming more open to new challenges and bigger dreams.

Eric's Journals

December 17, 2009

Today was really fun. You guys made this year my best birthday ever!!! It was a great lunch with all the volunteers. I had fun talking to Autumn. I wish I would have had the life way back when, for you all help build a nicer supporting life for me this year. Thank you for letting me in the program, I am having so much fun!!

Spring 2010

R4R means the world to me. The program has build my self esteem back up that was lost quite a while ago. It has built friendships. Most off it has given me the love of riding again. Thanks to R4R I am better around people and I look at myself much greater than I used to.

December 2, 2010

I'm proud of myself for helping this program. I am also proud of myself for being a leader. I think I've come a long way since last year. I owe so much to all of you for me turning into who I am today. You have kept a close eye on me and have protected me when I've needed protecting. I am also proud of my partner Wayne he is becoming a real leader.

Spring 2011

At the end of the day. I feel wonderful not only do I feel I need a shower. But I feel accomplished like I changed a life.

Jack I was so happy to see get engaged in today's activities. He really started to come out and show his personality. I'm sure you remember the kid I talked about when I taught mentally disabled kids how to play tennis. Up until last week I felt he was my greatest accomplishment. Now I feel Jack could become my biggest accomplishment. Is that wrong?

Final Journal Entry—Spring 2011

> This program has changed my entire life almost. It's filled a lonely empty feeling I used to have. This program has showed me people do care. You just have to look. This year at a point I felt helpless when they said it was possible that I had cancer, but Wally helped me through it. I want to thank all my teachers an principal for being there for me. I also want to thank my fellow R4R students and volunteers at the farm for supporting me.

Chapter 12

Mariah Nate Fund

When an organization opens its doors for a group of twenty unruly teenagers and rambunctious middle-schoolers, it's not without its risks. Organizations assuming this responsibility are made well aware of the challenges and hazards this imposes. Reaching for the Reins, though, has been extremely fortunate to have been blessed by multiple people and organizations that have unconditionally embraced them, challenges and all, and given them the opportunity to shine. As a result of this genuine acceptance and the opportunities they are provided, I felt from the very beginning the importance of incorporating an additional element of giving back into the program, something beyond our normal farm routine. I understand this may sound redundant, because the students are already giving their time, but it was always my goal to show them there are innumerable ways both to give and to experience the benefits of giving.

During the first two years of the program we worked with nonprofit organizations, whose self-support occasionally imposed certain financial challenges, so the students decided to give back by hosting several fund-raisers. With unrestrained enthusiasm they sold flowers for Valentine's Day and pizza at lunch, always brainstorming other methods to raise money. The students had a wonderful time spreading the word about their fund-raising to their friends and family, and their involvement showed their investment in the giving. When we'd raised enough funds, we contacted the local feed mill and farm supply store to see if they would give us a discount to make the students' efforts stretch as far as possible. The students purchased grain, wormer, horse treats, brushes, and other horse care products.

The presentation of the gifts was magical. The students huddled around the back of the SUV as I went to find the director and barn manager. As they approached the kids, they knew something was up, and with a flourish we opened the hatch to reveal the grain and several oddly wrapped but colorful packages. With tears in their eyes they read the students' cards and began opening the lovingly wrapped packages containing the horse supplies. But more important than the gifts themselves was the act of freely giving something without any strings attached. The gifts received by the students from having been able to help others were clearly the most important received that day.

When the program transitioned to Circle "C" Stable, a for-profit farm, fund-raising to help supply the farm with needed materials no longer made sense. This created a new opportunity for students to develop a plan to spend their fund-raising money to thank the farm for the opportunities they had been given.

Mariah

Cindy started riding horses when she was five and started showing when she was nine. But the horse that started it all did not come into her life until she was in seventh grade. Mariah was the only foal ever born on her parents' farm, and she was Cindy's pride and joy. Under Cindy's guidance and training, the red roan grew into a well-mannered 4-H show horse.

When Cindy left home to attend Western Michigan University to study teaching, her circumstances forced her to sell Mariah, though she did so with the understanding that she had the first option to buy her back if the buyer ever decided to sell her. As time passed, Cindy graduated from college but did not become a teacher. Instead, because she was disenchanted with the politics in education, she went to work for Cal, the father of one of her close 4-H friends and a local contractor. For fifteen years she worked construction during the day and kept horses as a hobby. As Cal started to think about retirement, Cindy found herself giving more and more horseback riding lessons at a local barn. This was when Cal approached Cindy with an idea.

Shortly thereafter, Cal cosigned loans for Cindy to finance the construction of her own barns in order to combine her love of horses with her talents as a teacher. At the time she already had about thirty students, so in March 2001, she built her barns and slowly started putting more time into Circle "C" Stable and less time into the construction business. Once the business was financially sustainable, Cal transitioned from contracting to become Cindy's maintenance man.

In the meantime, Cindy was able to buy Mariah back, and she quickly became her number-one lesson horse. Mariah's incredible intuitiveness and her ability to adapt to the strengths and weaknesses of her riders made her the best lesson horse Cindy has ever had, confidently transporting riders from four to seventy years of age. Cindy describes Mariah as having possessed a special sense for reading people, and it was evident she knew when she needed to be gentle and when she needed to push them.

Mariah was both Cindy's partner in her adventure of starting Circle "C" Stable and her backbone for sustaining the farm. Their connection was unmistakable to all who were lucky enough to experience the pair in action. When Cindy rode Mariah, it was a picture-perfect match, as if horse and rider were of a single mind. Their bond in everyday life was sweet and comical as well. At dinnertime Cindy would open Mariah's paddock gate, and she would obediently walk the fifty yards to the barn and down the row of stall doors to her own stall. When she finished eating, Cindy would call out, "Aren't you going to say thank you?" Mariah would respond with a sweet nicker. Throughout the day, if Cindy were ever in her vicinity, Mariah would paw at the stall door, making it bang and clatter, asking for seconds. On occasion it worked, and so she kept up the ritual.

Mariah's participation in the Reaching for the Reins program was far too brief. She was twenty-eight years old and had developed arthritis in her front end to the point where she was unsteady on her feet and stumbled at times and lost her balance. Because of this, she was no longer able to help with lessons. In December 2009, it became evident she was experiencing a lot of pain, and her hind end was giving out with the added strain of compensating for the arthritis. Cindy made the tough call to give her friend the peace she had so lovingly earned through the years, and she was laid to rest at the bottom of a hill near a grove of pine trees.

Nate

A gentle giant is the best way to describe Nate. Those uncomfortable around horses might find a sixteen-hand horse imposing, but this chestnut gelding was anything but intimidating. Pat acquired Nate when he was twenty-four years old. Even though he had some health issues, mainly arthritis in his front end, she was drawn to his personality and gladly accepted the responsibility of taking over his care and upkeep. Pat had owned four previous horses and had bred one of her mares three times, but Nate was different than any others she had ever owned. He was one of those rare horses whose gaze gave the impression he was looking into your soul. The eager-to-please giant did anything requested of him and in return only asked for jellybeans and a good brush down, and would often peer over his shoulder while being groomed as if to thank you for taking such good care of him.

The first year at Circle "C" Stable the students immediately fell in love with Nate. He was the go-to horse for EAL activities as well as a favorite for students learning to ride. That year more than half of the students in the program experienced their first ride on a horse from Nate. No matter how scared they initially were, there was a prevailing sense that no matter what happened, he would keep them safe.

Nate had a way of endearing himself to anyone around him. Perhaps it was his steady-as-a-rock personality or the way he seemed to be able to give a hug by laying his head over your shoulder or swinging it around your body to rest it on your chest. Perhaps it was the way he looked at people and seemed to *know* them. Whatever it was, Nate was a cornerstone on which the students built their horse skills and developed their confidence that first year.

In late January 2010, I received an e-mail from Pat requesting I inform the students of a sudden situation involving Nate. I gathered the students in my room and explained to them that, over the weekend, Nate was no longer able to support himself with his hind end. For many hours he'd tried to stand, but each time he couldn't seem to get control of his muscles. During his struggle he called out to Lightning in the adjoining stall, with whom he'd also shared a paddock, as if to reassure his friend. Cindy and Pat were his constant companions through the night, but as morning broke it was evident he was beyond help. Understanding she owed her friend the benefit of a painless passage on his last adventure, Pat sent him to run on that eternal rolling plain, free of the encumbrances of this world.

I read Pat's e-mail to the students through the lump in my throat and with tears in my eyes. I was not the only one struggling with my emotions. Even one of the tough guys, who sports a spiderweb tattoo on his elbow, shed a few tears that afternoon. He had worked with Nate every single week we attended the farm and mourned the loss of his companionship.

As I read her e-mail, it was evident the intent was not just to let the students know what happened but also to encourage them about Nate's life and struggle. Nate had not given up even when in the midst of an ongoing painful struggle. Up to the end he still wanted to be that gentle giant, reassuring his friend Lightning and companion Pat, and modeling courage to all those who worked with him.

The Gift

The students in the Reaching for the Reins program realized from the first moment that they stepped off the bus at Circle "C" Stable that they were being given a tremendous opportunity. As they thought about what to do with the funds they'd raised, it was their prevailing desire to provide to others a similar opportunity of what they'd experienced. From this vision the Mariah Nate Fund was born.

On February 18, 2010, the students presented Cindy and Pat with $475 from their fund-raising efforts to start the Mariah Nate Fund in honor of the two horses that changed so many lives. The mission statement the students created for the fund was, "To benefit special riders." They wanted to ensure that others would be able to experience the same opportunities they were given at Circle "C" Stable. Cindy and Pat were both blown away and had tears in their eyes during the presentation. Their joy and appreciation created a moment for the students they will never forget.

Each year since, the students have added to the Mariah Nate Fund, and Cindy has honored their wishes by using it to help very special riders experience magical moments with horses. She is currently using the fund to supplement a young girl's riding lessons whose family is experiencing several financial difficulties. The girl has autism, cerebral palsy, and some additional cognitive impairment. The family was discussing changing her lessons to a biweekly schedule instead of weekly, but they knew this would create significant problems in her ability to retain what she learned and continue the positive progress she was making. When Cindy talked to them about their situation, she offered to supplement part of every other week's lessons with the Mariah Nate funds so that the girl could continue with her weekly lessons and continue making positive gains. These are precisely the kinds of experiences the Reaching for the Reins students wanted to be able to provide for others.

* * *

February 18, 2010

Ava

> Seeing Cindy and Pat's faces when we gave them the gifts was great. Their faces were so happy and once again we started to tear up. It was nice.

Greg

> Today was sweet. I think it's awesome about the Mariah Nate Fund. It's great that we helped establish this for people who need help like special riders. It felt great to see Cindy and Pat's face when we presented the pictures and the money. It gave me a warm feeling of Joy to see their faces light up.

Nichole

> I think the Mariah Nate fund is a really great thing. They were so happy and shocked when we gave them the money and pictures.

Chapter 13

A Chicken Horse

We've all heard it said that laughter is the best medicine, and Cal makes it his mission to dispense that medicine by whatever means necessary and as often as possible. One thing that immediately strikes Cal when he meets both sets of students is the weight of the burdens each of them carries on their minds. Whether financial difficulties, family dysfunction, personal illness, or teenage strife, many of the students carry struggles that loom constantly in their minds, clouding their possibilities and diminishing their full potential.

Cal is determined to get the students beyond this cloud through laughter, even if only for a few short minutes. Most of the students describe him as the biggest kid on the farm. He often takes outrageous to a whole new level, and wherever he goes, laughter follows closely on his heels.

One of the ways we prep the Cedar Lane students for the arrival of the Lighthouse students is by having the volunteers pretend they know nothing about horses. This provides the Cedar Lane students the opportunity to put into practice their unconventional education, providing a real-world setting for vocalizing instruction, correcting behavior, and praising accomplishments. To test the degree of our students' resolve and discipline, the volunteers exaggerate the difficulties our students might encounter. Cal loves to be a student.

* * *

Cal was assigned as Phil and Samantha's student. As always, the Cedar Lane students-turned-instructors are taught to introduce themselves to their students. Then, before they begin working, the Cedar Lane instructors get the new students' helmets. Samantha, a junior with dark-brown hair and an enthusiastic personality, introduced herself first and shook Cal's hand. Then Phil, a sophomore with long, shaggy hair, introduced himself and led Cal to the tack area to get him a helmet. Cal immediately started in with his antics. He politely greeted Samantha and *Phyllis*. Naturally, Phil corrected him, but Cal was certain Phil's long hair was ample proof he was, in fact, a girl, and he was unwavering in this observation. After Cal was fitted with a helmet, the trio found their way back to Lightning's stall, where they instructed Cal on brushing a horse. Cal halfheartedly brushed the horse while the kids coaxed him through what each brush was for. Cal patiently awaited his next opportunity. As soon as both instructors momentarily looked away, Cal scooted out of the stall to chase one of the barn cats. Samantha, patiently and with a smile, brought him back to his task. No sooner did he have a brush in hand than he loudly announced he had to use the bathroom. The teens showed him where it was, and minutes later Cal emerged with wet hands, chattering about how the farm needed to warm up its toilet water because it made his hands cold when he tried to clean them in it. This sent Samantha into a fit of laughter while Phil, a tougher sell, merely grinned and shook his head. Again, they led Cal back to the stall, where he proceeded to ask Phyllis to be his girlfriend. Phil chuckled and politely turned him down. Little did Samantha and Phil suspect that Cal was just beginning to warm up.

As Phil escorted Cal down the aisle of the barn to get the saddle and saddle pad, Cal grabbed ahold of Phil's arm and announced to the onlookers that Phyllis was his new girlfriend. This was enough to drag a few unrestrained chuckles through Phil's smile, but he continued to shake his head. On the way back to the stall, Cal carried the saddle pad. As he shuffled along, he intentionally caught his left toe on the heel of his right boot and went sprawling. He conveniently cushioned his fall with the saddle pad and again caused the onlookers to chuckle.

I am not sure how, but despite Cal's intrepid challenges, Samantha and Phil finally taught him how to saddle. But once in the saddle, Cal proved to be a less than model student. He waved to other pretend students, dropped his reins, and kicked his feet out of his stirrups. Each time the group passed the gate, Samantha and Phil had a new story to tell.

* * *

James and Owen were Cal's chosen partners for the day. Cal's persona for the afternoon was a kid who loved to fight. His name was Muhammad Cal, a distant relative of Muhammad Ali. As they were grooming the horse, he continually talked of fighting and tried to pretend-punch the horse and anyone standing in his path. Both James and Owen reminded him multiple times that punching any horse was not acceptable, but Cal was persistent. Cal tried unsuccessfully to convince them that the barrel of the horse was for brushing but the hindquarters were for punching. Both Owen and James were easy targets and soon began laughing at whatever silliness Cal threw their way.

As they finished brushing the horse, Cal started to explain why this was not just a regular horse but a chicken horse. The root of his logic was in the fact that horses lay brown eggs. As soon as this declaration came to out of Cal's mouth, Owen burst out of the stall in a fit of belly laughter. With tears in his eyes and choking back his laughter, he explained to the onlookers what he had just experienced with Cal.

As Owen regained his composure and reentered the stall, Cal began explaining what he used chicken horse eggs for. He alleged that each morning he scrambled them for breakfast. Then, with a gloved hand, he reached down to show the boys how to collect the "eggs." In disbelief the teens howled in laughter at the lunacy of it, but as he grasped a misshapen nugget, they remembered their job was to keep Cal safe and prevent him from doing crazy things. This definitely counted as crazy. James calmly but with difficulty attempted to explain why picking up horse droppings was probably not the best way to occupy their time, but Owen again stepped out of the stall, unable to control his amusement at the outrageous hilarity of the situation.

Once in the saddle, Cal, who admittedly does not know much about horses, was trying to learn how to hold the reins. As the boys explained what to do, he continued to play, blissfully ignorant and tenaciously obstinate. As he positioned one hand correctly, the boys helped him place his other hand, and while the boys did this, he would change the first. After a few moments, more than three times the normal amount of time it should take, James stepped in and placed his hands over Cal's, showing him exactly what to do. Although Cal was being silly, James learned firsthand how to be eternally patient as well as a new way to teach.

* * *

On occasion, Cal's brother Wally is able to join the R4R group. As brothers do, Cal and Wally banter back and forth about all manner of silly childhood and adult memories. Wally lost his right arm to cancer several years ago, and one of their favorite stories to tell the students is about their trip to Alaska.

The brothers had always wanted to fly their small two-seater airplane to Alaska. Finally, a few years ago when the brothers were both in their sixties, they decided to make the dream come true. Many of their friends and family gathered for the takeoff from the hay field behind Cal's house. When Cal tells the story, he claims the large send-off was because no one thought they would return.

Their four-day trip was a success, and on the return flight to southwest Michigan, Cal was anxious to get home. The brothers had cabin fever being stuck in such a confining space together for so long, and they started to get a bit punchy. Cal decided he wanted to fly over the narrowest part of Lake Michigan instead of going around the lake as they had initially planned. The shortcut would save them several hours on their trip. Cal's reasoning was that, if they flew high enough and developed engine problems they could *probably* coast to the shore on the other side. Wally, clearly the more practical of the two, insisted that the plane was too small and that they would never make it to the other side. Cal's retort was that it would be fine because he would simply land on the water and they could swim to shore. Wally, not accustomed to letting Cal off the hook that easily, stated that swimming was all fine and good for Cal, but that with only one arm he would be stuck swimming in endless circles.

The brothers' shared sense of humor always keeps the students engaged, and even though there is usually a good lesson at the end of their stories, they coat it liberally with a heavy dose of laughter.

* * *

It is always challenging to come up with new and exciting things to do in the arena when the cold and rainy weather persists into the spring. One afternoon, Cindy gave Cal and Wally the task of setting up the indoor arena for the day's lesson. The brothers set off to accomplish the task with characteristic mischief.

As the groups of students with horses in tow entered the arena, the brothers proudly announced that they were entering a racetrack. They had transformed the arena into a track with cones, ground poles, and barrels. When the students began to ride, Cal and Wally began announcing. As students passed by the fence, they would ask if they needed new tires (horseshoes), and when the students went into a corner, the pair would make screeching tire sounds. Before long, the boys in the saddle were making engine and tire noises right along with the brothers and correlating the horses' actions to race car lingo. When a horse would stop, Cal and Wally would announce that an engine blew, or when the saddle got a bit loose and needed retightened they would equate it to a pit stop. The entire group was grinning from ear to ear as they played along with the scenario. The day's lesson flew by, and Cindy was barely given a chance to get a word in edgewise. The groups made lap after lap thinking of new terms and analogies to add to the event. Usually toward the end of the lesson the Cedar Lane students are showing signs of fatigue from walking or running lap after lap, but not this day. Their minds were kept active, and their energy remained high. When the lesson ended, they continued the playful game as they escorted their race cars back to their stalls to untack.

* * *

Students clamber to work with Cal. He always has a smile on his face, and he works hard to transfer it to others. Even if only for a few moments, the natural ease of his presence helps them forget their difficulties and removes the clouds of worry from their minds so they can make a few memories, enjoy a meaningful experience, and indulge in the best medicine good company can offer.

Chapter 14

Never Forget This Place

I love it when the volunteers' minds start racing! In mid-November the students participated in a new EAL activity where they were asked to pick three events in their lives that they would encounter in the next six months that might be difficult. They picked school, Christmas break, and graduation. Many of the volunteers, who come from a different world context, were hung up on the concept of Christmas and how it could possibly be something unpleasant. Curious, they asked the students what about Christmas made it difficult. The students shared with them their differing experiences that culminated in a very dreary picture of what the holidays are really like for some people. It was not the lack of gifts that the students were worried about; it was much more than that.

Many students thrive under the structure that school provides—there are two guaranteed meals a day, fighting is not tolerated, and there are few surprises. Conversely, at home and on the streets, these are not guarantees. Some students shared that they may face a lack of food at home over the holidays, while others talked about the family fights or the all-day drinking parties that have become the norm of holiday functions.

The revelations shared by the students were what sent the volunteers' minds racing. After the students left for the day, they had a meeting and decided to surprise them the last day they came to the farm before Christmas break. For two weeks before the event, they told the kids they'd better make sure to attend on December 22. I joined in the fun as well and hyped up the day every chance I could. Many of the students started to hound me to tell them what the day had in store, but I merely smiled and told them they'd have to wait and see. The waiting drove them crazy, and they began to try to bribe us all for clues.

Finally, three days before Christmas, we loaded onto the bus and headed for the farm. The kids were understandably excited about what was in store, and many of them pestered me for details the entire half-hour ride. Even though Michigan did not send snow for Christmas this particular year, the spirit was still in the air.

When the bus arrived, the students spilled out and rushed down the stairs to Cindy's basement to see what the day held in store for them. When they reached the landing, they were met with tables decorated with red paper and several mysterious containers carefully piled up on various tables. After several minutes of excited jostling and with much prompting, they finally settled down and quieted enough for us to explain what we would be doing for the day. Cindy explained to them we would be having a Christmas celebration complete with food, cutting down and decorating a Christmas tree, making ornaments, and decorating cookies. This might not be exciting for most high school kids, but they were elated. It didn't take long for them to immerse themselves elbow-deep in one activity or another.

When Cal asked who wanted to go help him cut down the Christmas tree, he was met with ten eager offers. As the group tromped to the edge of Cindy's property to pick out their tree, several of them were extremely excited, chattering about how they had never gone out to cut down a tree before or how they had never had a real tree. The group walked up and down the row of twenty trees twice, inspecting and commenting on each one before they selected their perfect tree. Cal started the cut but soon handed the saw to one of the students eager to experience it firsthand. After a few minutes, he in turn handed it to another. This was truly a joint effort. Once the timber fell, another set of hands grabbed the branches and carried it to the house. After some prep work in the garage to fit the tree into the stand, they triumphantly carried their prize down to the basement.

Gina, another of our volunteers, came up with several clever ideas on how to make cards and tree ornaments. One of the ornaments was shaped like a horse, which fit perfectly with our horse-crazy program. So while the first group was getting the tree, a second group wasted no time in making cards for their families, along with colorful paper chains, horse ornaments, and snowflakes to hang on the tree. As soon as the tree gang returned, they too joined in the festivities. As the decorations were finished, the students quickly filled the branches with their handiwork.

Once the tree was well under way, another group started decorating cookies. The volunteers had all pitched in and made several dozen cookies along with icing, and provided a multitude of decorating materials. The group formed an assembly line where Mrs. East iced cookies, and the students decorated. They all sat at one long table and passed down the assembly chain the type of cookies and icing they wanted.

At one point, Cal staged a rebellion and, having enlisted a small band of students, cornered Cindy while the students smeared a bit of icing on her cheek. The plan worked well and sent the group into a fit of laughter.

By the time the tree was fully decorated, complete with lights and colorful handmade expressions of teamwork, and all the cookies were either iced, eaten, or both, it was time for lunch. The volunteers had collaborated to create a spread of food, including potato casserole, chicken, salads, and pie. For some of the students, this might be the best meal they would have until returning to school after Christmas. The group sat together devouring plate after plate of home-cooked goodness, all the while enjoying each other's company.

One of the students struck up a conversation with Gina during lunch. The student expressed how family get-togethers with her family were nothing like this. They always revolved around drinking, and family members were always too drunk to share in the good times and fun activities. With a far-off look in her eyes, she vowed that when she had children their lives would be different—that she would provide them with happy memories like this around the holidays.

As everyone finished the last plates of food, the atmosphere was festive and happy, and it was evident the Reaching for the Reins group was a family. As if the experience up to this point was not good enough, Cindy explained that it was time to hand out gifts. In the corner was a huge pile of colorfully wrapped packages that had been sitting there since the students' arrival. Because the students were unaccustomed to such lavish experiences, they were completely unassuming in thinking the gifts were for them. Cindy and Cal donned a set of reindeer antlers and a Santa hat and, along with the rest of the volunteers, began passing out the gifts.

Each student received a personalized stocking, card, and several wrapped packages. They sat staring at them for a few moments and, only when they were assured it was okay to open them, tore into them with smiles and wide eyes. Some tore into every package as fast as they could to see what each held, while others took their time reading each word of the card before they carefully inspected their packages. They each received a sweatshirt, gloves, hat, scarf, blanket, socks, and a stocking full of goodies. In true teenage fashion, most immediately donned their new apparel, complimenting each other on their new look. One of the students quietly took off his shoes, revealing bare feet. He put on the new socks he'd just received and with a smile put his shoes back on. Even though his actions had been subtle, Gina had to turn away to mask the tears in her eyes.

When asked about their favorite moments from the 2011–12 Reaching for the Reins program, all of the volunteers included the Christmas party on their list. Each of them expressed how Christmas that year was made complete three days before December 25. The joy that comes from spending time together happened for each of them with their Reaching for the Reins family, all huddled together in the warmth of fellowship and goodwill in the happiest basement in southwest Michigan.

* * *

December 22, 2011

Mark

> I am grateful for all my friend and family. They both mean a lot to me. So I try not to take things for granted and be more appreciative for things. Today was an amazing day at the farm. Cal was smearing icing on Cindy and the gifts were great! Thank you Circle C Stables! Also the food hit the spot.

Derek W

> It was a fun day at Reaching for the Reins. We cut down a real tree, decorated it and made decorations and decorated cookies. We had a feast and got a few presents that came in handy. Actually I am thankful that we all celebrated as a group. Today was the best day in a while.

Claire

> Today I had a wonderful day. First thing I will say is thank you Mrs. Carlsen for letting me back in the program. I won't let you down this time. I love how everyone acted like a family. It feels like a family. Thank you so much I really appreciate it. Love Claire

Eric

> I liked everything about today. Definitely made my week. I'll miss Reaching for the Reins. It's hard to think this is my last year. But then again I think about how I can't wait for graduation. Today made me very happy, got my mind eased about a lot. Also made me realize how much I'll miss everyone.

Brandon M

Today was awesome day. We cut down a tree, made cookies, ate an awesome lunch and got gifts. I was so shocked about it. I didn't know the gifts were for us. I wished I wasn't sick but I try my best so to do everything we did today.

I am grateful for having awesome friends, funny teachers and a new life for me and being in the group I'm glad I'm in it and glad I'm doing an awesome job. I am grateful for my step mom, dad and brother and sister and that I am not in the house with my mom's crazy family anymore.

Sarah

I'm thankful for everyone on the farm and everything that has happened today. I wish we all could have got you all something besides our bright smiles. Today was overall fun with everyone. By the way almost everything is better at home. Mom's boyfriend is soon to be employed. Thank you all for the presents. These are the only ones I am going to get this year, but I know presents are not the most important. You're all my biggest and best presents ever.

Greg

I am grateful for the people in my life that care about me. Also for the things I do have. Today was great. We made ornaments for the tree, decorated cookies, made Christmas cards, got to enjoy seeing everyone have fun. We ate fried chicken, which is the best, for lunch. After that we opened up the gifts the volunteers got for us. It was awesome what they did. The really do care. It's not what they do it is that they thought about us. That makes me feel really good inside. It was a total surprise today. I didn't expect any of it. I am really thankful for everyone that thought about me.

Like most of the volunteers remember my allergies (Dairy & Eggs).

Amanda

Today was good. I enjoyed my time there. It was really nice of all of them what they did for us. It was cool. I liked making the ring thing that goes around the tree. Evan and I did started it. Decorating cookies was fun as well. God bless everyone at the Circle C Stable.

One thing I am thankful for would be my life, friends, my boyfriend, my best friend Evan, and my family! (:

Phil

Today we went and cut down a Christmas Tree. Then we decorated it with hand made decorations. We also decorated cookies to take home. We each to a few gifts. Thanks to all the staff.

So thank you, we really appreciate everything that you have done for us in the past and future.

Evan

We had a lil party today. We made cookies and me and Bobby cut down the tree. Me and Amanda started making the ring thing to wrap around the tree but Alice and Carie finished them. I made a horse. We also ate so much food I am still full right now and the food was so good I had to get seconds. The volunteers bought everyone of us gifts for Christmas and I am so thankful for them and everything else. I learned from them and had a great year. So this is my last journal I am going to write this year. We'll the rest of 2011 and I am looking forward to seeing everyone in the new year.

Jennifer

Today was really great! I really wasn't expecting anything in return for just being able to be around horses on Thursday is enough for me. But I'm really grateful that I got stuff for Christmas because Lakoda ripped my gloves. LOL and now I have got like 5 new pair and 2 hats.

Alice

Today was very nice. I really wasn't expecting any of it. Today we went down to Cindy's basement and she threw us a Christmas party. I am very thankful for that. We decorated a tree (that we cut down there). We decorated cookies and also had a feast.

The one thing I would have to say I'm thankful for is the ones whom love me. My family and friends. I'm thankful I have a house and everything.

Carie

Today was amazing. I wasn't expecting everyone to do all that stuff for us. I wouldn't have ever guessed that we would get all these gifts. They are amazing and it's a lot more that what I would ever thought to get. Today was overall the best day because I feel like everyone bonded one way or another. I loved getting our own tree and making cookies and ornaments. I am very thankful for everything you guys have done for me and everyone else it means a lot to me. Thanks for everything. Carie

Chapter 15

Spreading Joy

Eric has a compelling need to help people. This is what makes him feel good about himself and is one of the things that helps him put one foot in front of the other when times get tough. It was his third and last year in Reaching for the Reins, and he was excited for the Lighthouse boys to join the program.

Thomas came to Lighthouse a quiet student uninterested in participating in group activities or socializing with peers. His life experiences had left him with social anxiety, and he struggled to trust others or seek out spontaneous conversation. However, Thomas looked forward to the farm and Eric.

Partnerships at the farm are very important. The teachers create profiles for each of the students and then put them in groups to try to match personalities and ability levels. Teachers and volunteers work extremely hard pairing students together who highlight each other's strengths and who enable each other to develop. The first week at the farm everyone monitors each group to see how well they work with each other, and adjustments are made to ensure that everyone gets the most out of the experience.

When Thomas came to Lighthouse he never initiated a conversation, and when spoken to he would respond with as little as possible, often with only a single word. He always chose to sit away from everyone and tried his utmost to remain unnoticed. Like many in the Cedar Lane population, Thomas had been bullied in the past by students at previous schools, which made him untrusting of the world around him. To survive, he learned to remain extremely quiet and became introverted. Because of Eric's similar background, we felt he and Thomas might best be able to relate to each other. As months passed, he began to open up a bit to his five other Lighthouse classmates, but if left to do what he was truly comfortable with, he chose isolation without fail.

* * *

Eric and Thomas hit it off right from the beginning. Eric's patience and persistence helped Thomas get through the moments where he was frustrated and did not want to try something new. The first week, Thomas was very unsure about riding, but Eric and Mrs. Olson, Thomas's teacher, talked him through his fears and got him into the saddle. As Eric led him around the arena several times, he continued to check with him on how he was feeling and reassure him that he would keep him safe.

However, after two weeks of riding Thomas suddenly decided that he was done riding. Regardless of how much coaxing Eric, Cindy, and Mrs. Olson provided, he refused to ride. Even though he did not want to ride, Mrs. Olson felt it was important for him to try something new every week. Under Mrs. Olson's guidance, Thomas set goals for himself, and Eric celebrated each success he accomplished.

Thomas spent his first week off the horse walking up and down the mounting block. In subsequent weeks he progressed to putting one foot in the stirrup and putting some weight in the saddle. Even though he was making progress toward riding again, he still refused to take the final steps and swing into the saddle.

Interaction with the horses seemed to be a very positive thing for Thomas's self esteem, and so, after his practice session, he would walk Clark, a large white gelding, around the arena. The first time Eric accompanied him for a few laps, showing him how to stop and turn. Then Eric handed over the lead rope and watched in pride as Thomas ambled around lap after lap. Clark seemed to know that he had a novice leader and responded as gently as an animal his size is able, dropping his head nearly to the ground and plodding around a few paces behind Thomas, whose proud smile was visible across the arena.

* * *

The third week of Thomas's refusal to ride was also alumni day. Several students from former Reaching for the Reins years, both from Cedar Lane and Lighthouse, joined the current year's group at the farm for the day's activities. Alumni day is always a special time for catching up with old friends and making new ones.

Each year Cindy ensures there is time for all of the alumni to work with the students and horses and, if they choose, to ride. It always warms my heart when I hear the Cedar Lane students' first priority for the day is not riding or working with the horses but working with the students. The feeling they get from helping others is what they truly desire out of their visit back to the farm.

Since the day was filled with a surplus of students, Eric and Thomas acquired two Cedar Lane alumni in their group, Natalie and Andrew. The trio first helped Thomas saddle up Clark and then made their way to the outdoor arena to ride. Thomas was quick to inform the group of his protest to riding. Andrew assured him that he was not the only person who was anxious about riding, that even older guys like him had a bit of fear.

The day was gorgeous. The sun blazed high overhead, and the breeze carried a fresh apple blossom scent from the nearby orchard across the open arena. One group after another helped their riders into the saddle and headed to the white picket rail. After a couple of practice laps, they began weaving in and out of orange cones and standing up in the stirrups while crossing over logs.

Thomas's group was the last to arrive in the arena. Thomas gingerly entered the arena and began his slow, methodical march up the mounting block. With a degree of uncertainty, he stuck one foot in the stirrup and put a little weight in the saddle. Then back down the mounting block he came. After several more rounds he declared that he had done more than during the previous week and that he was done.

Believing this lone act didn't fully showcase Thomas's accomplishments at the farm, Cindy suggested Thomas help Andrew ride. Andrew, a tall, slender twenty-year-old with his hat turned backward and sporting dark sunglasses and a goatee, might normally have been intimidating to the young man, but Thomas had found safety at the farm. At Cindy's suggestion a smile crossed Thomas's face, and he took ahold of the situation with purpose. Thomas instinctively began to mimic everything Eric had taught him about how to get on the horse. Suddenly the authority, Thomas took control of the situation, instructing Andrew on where to put his feet on each of the steps and which foot to put in the stirrup. One step at a time, Andrew followed his directions. Andrew continued to insist that he was a bit scared, and Thomas gently encouraged him, telling him, "You can do it." As soon as Andrew swung his leg over the saddle, Thomas started to clap and, triumphantly and with an enormous smile on his face, declared, "You did it!"

By way of affirming Andrew's success, Thomas took ahold of the lead rope and led Clark and Andrew around the arena. After a few steps he looked back at Andrew and asked him how he was feeling and whether he was okay. Andrew assured him that he felt safe as long as Thomas was his leader. Thomas puffed out his chest in pride. Natalie fell in step on the opposite side of Clark to ensure he behaved himself. When he tried to go the wrong way, she subtly corrected him so that Thomas did not see and could assume he was solely responsible for their success. Eric sat on the mounting block in the center of the arena proudly watching his protégé step up from being an intimidated rider to a confident leader.

The communication skills and confidence Thomas portrayed were unprecedented. Not only did he initiate the interaction, he did not stop with just a word or two. He openly interacted with and affirmed Andrew, giving him the details he needed to get on the horse and praising him for his success. This moment propelled Thomas into a new role at the farm.

Each week thereafter, Thomas insisted on helping someone else ride. He talked all week at school about how good a teacher he was and how he could help others get over their fears. Eric, week after patient week, helped Thomas saddle Clark and then proudly watched as he helped others in the arena.

The final week of the program that year was no different. Thomas and Eric went through their preliminary routine and then headed to the arena. Evan, a Cedar Lane student, was assigned as Thomas's rider for the day. But Thomas had a different idea. Instead, Thomas insisted that on his last week he wanted to lead his teacher around. Eric swung into the saddle with pride, and the two buddies took their final laps for the year around the arena in reversed roles. Thomas had learned a lot from Eric about working with the horses, but the most important lesson Eric passed to Thomas was the joy that comes from helping others, a feeling that can help overcome even the toughest barriers and fears.

* * *

The last day of the program always starts with students spending time together looking through their yearbooks and writing messages to each other. This is Eric's final journal entry from that day.

May 3, 2012

> It feels great to be in a yearbook so people can look back and say I know that guy. Also having a yearbook with signatures and notes. It's one way of knowing my life has meant something to others this far. I love going back in my old yearbooks seeing what people had to say compared to my current one. To see if I grew up any. My favorite memory this year in the program is from today. Thomas wanted to be my leader. This program has helped me realize I can be worth something to this huge world.

Chapter 16

Sit Tall in the Saddle

Ninety-five pounds of peace, patience, joy, understanding, and compassion—that's how I see Cora. Perhaps one of the slightest people I've ever had the pleasure of knowing, she is one of the most resilient people I have ever met. While her life's story gives her ample reason to be frustrated, angry, and depressed, she chooses instead to stay positive and joyful and make the best out of every situation.

Cora came to Cedar Lane her senior year because she was behind on credits. Admittedly, the credit deficit was due to a number of poor choices she'd made. She was expelled from school her sophomore year for popping pills in the hallway and missed the second half of her junior year when she ran off to Arkansas with her boyfriend. When her senior year rolled around, she was determined to knuckle down and conquer her last year of high school.

Cora is an extremely articulate young woman whose journal entries give insight into the mind and strength of an eighteen-year-old girl who has lived through a lifetime of trials in a very short time. The following is Cora's Reaching for the Reins journal. I have introduced many of her entries to help paint the whole picture of her journey at Cedar Lane and through the R4R program. Some of the entries will stand on their own merit without any introduction.

October 1, 2009

Our first day at Reaching for the Reins was really cool. We got to learn how to clean a stall (a little), and watch the horses interact with each other. I didn't do too well at shoveling poo because I didn't have my contacts in so I couldn't see it. I had fun watching the horses, but I wish I could have petted them more. I really like the dogs that are at the farm too. They're so cute! And we got to pet them! Work on the fence was way more physically exerting than it should have been. Or at least more tiring than I though it would be!

October 8, 2009

Today at the farm rocked! I was glad that I got to be with Brittney most of the time. She knows a lot about horses, so she was able to help me out a lot. We got to learn to groom the horses and lead the horses. I had fun grooming the horses, and I was surprised at how many different kinds of brushes could be used. I also liked leading the horses, but one of them totally freaked me out! It walked straight up to me from across the stable and tried to eat me! I don't know if it actually tried to bite me or if it wanted to lick me and was just being friendly, but it freaked me out! I wasn't taking any chances!

* * *

After participating in the blindfolded trust EAL, the students were encouraged to reflect on the experience.

October 15, 2009

I don't really trust people very easily. That's why it's easier to trust animals. They're usually very sweet, they just need love and attention. I trust my close friends and my teachers. Oh, and close family. But with animals, I don't feel like I have to be as picky. They never have a motive (except sometimes they do want treats) and they never really try to hurt you in any way. They listen to you and they don't argue, or try to hurt your feelings. That's why I love animals. For me to trust someone, I think that I just have to get to know them. If I know them for a long time, and they never tried to hurt me, or they've proved that they are a good friend then I know I can trust them. With animals, I trust them from the get to. But if an animal is mean, I will lose trust in it.

* * *

As a child, Cora had severe medical challenges. She was born with several holes in her heart and had to see a cardiologist every six months for checkups. Generally, these holes close over time, but hers were slow to close. The holes in her heart, coupled with her asthma, restricted her physical activity as she grew up, and she was not allowed to go outside when it was below forty degrees.

These, however, were not the biggest of her medical challenges, which her grandfather was quick to point out. His only concern with her being in Reaching for the Reins was her back. Cora, who views the world through a curiously positive lens, recalls being delighted when she discovered at thirteen that one shoulder was higher than the other. This set off warning flags for her grandmother, who suffered from scoliosis, a curvature of the spine. One doctor's visit later, she was diagnosed with extreme scoliosis. The curvature was so severe it required the surgical insertion of a permanent metal rod in her back. However, because this surgery could overstress her heart, she first had to undergo heart surgery to close the persisting holes.

Between the two surgeries and recovery, she was out of school for more than six months during her seventh-grade year. Not only did these medical ordeals make it difficult for her to keep pace with the rest of her class that year, they were also very painful. As a result, she has had to be extremely careful with her back. With great concern and compassion, her grandfather asked that I pay close attention to her at the farm. He emphasized that I make sure she was careful with how much physical labor she performed and how much weight she lifted. I assured him I would, and from the first time I saw her ride I noticed that as a result of her medical history she had impeccable posture in the saddle.

October 21, 2009

> Today was so fun! I was so scared before I started riding. I wasn't really scared about getting bucked off, because I had Nate, and he seems way too nice to do anything like that. But I was worried that I would fall off somehow. When I got on, I was really nervous. But they told me to relax, so I took a deep breath and relaxed all of my muscles. It took a little time to get used to, but once I did it was really fun. I totally trust Nate. I kept accidently holding the reins the wrong way, but I think I understand now. I got to groom Moe for the first time today, too. Mrs. Carlson helped me and taught me how to clean the hooves. That was neat but pretty difficult. We even threw all the firewood out. Today was a busy day, but I had so much fun!

* * *

One of the more challenging but fun EAL activities we use to teach the group to function as a team starts by having students grouped in pairs of four in the arena with a loose horse. They are tasked with assigning two Thinkers and two Doers for the group. All members of the group are required to interlink their arms with the Thinkers in the middle, bookended by Doers on the outside. Then they are tasked with catching and saddling a horse. The challenge, though, is that the Doers on the outside are only permitted to do what the Thinkers in the middle tell them, and the Thinkers are only allowed to provide vocal instruction.

Four horses were ambling around the arena when Cora and her classmates entered to attempt the task. Two groups very quickly approached the two more docile horses, haltered them, and brought them to the fence for saddling. The other two horses were geldings and provided a far greater challenge. Geldings by nature are much more playful than mares, and they saw the gangly group of teenagers marching toward them as a game. They trotted self-assuredly from one end of the arena to the other, kicking up their heels with delight. When Cora's group managed to nearly corner one gelding, he threw up his head and softly cantered through the narrow opening between the students and the arena wall, throwing a horse smile over his shoulder. At one point the horses teamed up to use their herd mentality to work against the two groups of students trying to catch them. After this charade continued for about ten minutes, Cindy stepped forward and gave the horses "the look." This action went unnoticed by the students, but the horses immediately subdued and, even though they continued to put up a bit of a fight, they settled down and allowed themselves to be caught. As tends to be the case with people forced to rely on each other, the students struggled a bit to work together on saddling but finally managed the task after a lot of collaborative thinking.

The discussion following this EAL centers on teamwork, leadership, and communication. The Doers vented their frustrations about how difficult it was to know what they were doing but to have to rely on the instructions of the Thinkers for their group. The Thinkers confessed the challenge of articulating their knowledge of the task into understandable instruction.

October 29, 2009

> We were sooo late getting to the farm. But I had fun riding in Mrs. Carlson's car! It's really nice. When we got to the farm, were told we were going to clean out horse troffs (sp?). I couldn't do much because most of it would've hurt my back. And my back has been hurting all day anyway, or I might've still tried. But I still got to pour the water in and pet Taz (the barn cat). At the same time! Taz is so cute. I filled up two troffs, then went inside the pit with the horses. I got a group with Sarah, Derek, and Joel. Travis is the only person in the group I didn't really know. We got our instructions, and then tried to get our horse. That was easier said than done. It took, like, 10 minutes before we got one. The harness (halter) was not problem. The girth? That was a whole different story. We didn't even get that done until it was almost time to leave.

* * *

I often prompt the students to highlight their strengths in their journals. Far too often, teens spend the bulk of their time dwelling on their awkwardness or shortcomings. This particular week I asked the students to tell me something they do well or something positive they bring to the program.

November 5, 2009

Today was the most fun yet! I had so much fun! I got to ride Maggie, and she listens so well! Every time I told her to stop, she would stop, and when I told her to go she would go. I love riding Maggie. I felt so comfortable, I felt almost like I could do anything with her! It was as comfy as Nate, except Maggie's smaller. I think that's what makes me so comfy. I just love that horse!

I think my optimism is one of my best traits I can bring to this program. It's good because I'm pretty relaxed around the horses. I really hope to bring some optimism to the lives of some of the kids we get to see. I want to show them the good things in life and teach them to smile. I can't wait.

* * *

Sometimes, Reaching for the Reins is just about spending time with friends. One of my fondest memories is when, as a group, we spent the entire two and a half hours following lunch painting the fence around the outdoor arena. Most people probably wouldn't consider painting fun, but we had a blast talking and interacting with each other. This task gave the students, teachers, and volunteers an opportunity to talk outside the constraints of structured exercises and get to know each other better. As a teacher, an academic agenda always drives your interaction with the students. While you may be able to steal a few minutes here and there to get to know students, it is rare to have several hours of unabridged time to learn about their lives, interests, and goals.

November 12, 2009

> We didn't do too much today. We all got to eat, then we went and painted the fence. I thought painting was fun. It was a learning experience for me because I had never painted before. Well, other than art class, I suppose. Today I learned that Sarah is a good person to talk to. Hmmm ... I'll probably still give her a hard time though ... Teehee! Love my friendships!

* * *

One of the ways Cedar Lane students prepare to work with the Lighthouse students is to have volunteers pretend to be students themselves. These challenge-sessions give the Cedar Lane students much-needed practice working as a group and explaining instructions in detail. In addition, the students learn what it feels like to be in charge and mentor another person through a new process. It also allows the volunteers to give the students suggestions and compliment their developing skills.

November 19, 2009

> Today was fun. We got pizza, which was really good, and pop. I ate soo much. I did eat a good 5 pieces and a few cookies. I was stuffed!

> A hero in my life is my grandfather. I love him so much. He does a lot and has lived through a lot. He's 64 and he still works 6 days a week, for at least 5½ hours a day.

> But he still comes home and takes care of me, himself, and the house. He does so much. I don't know how he does it.

Teaching was more fun than I though it would be. At first it was a little weird, because I knew I was explaining things to her that she not only already knew, but probably knew better than me. She gave me really great advice on how to explain things to the kids, and what to watch out for. When I heard what she said, I felt really proud. She gave me more credit than I deserved, though, because a lot of what I did came from her guidance. She is really cool.

* * *

When Christy shared her story, the students were encouraged to use their journals to reflect on what they perceived her message to be.

December 3, 2009

Today we went back over saddling and grooming. I think I always forget the name of the brushes. And I'm happy because I'm finally starting to get better at cinching the knot on the girth. I had a lot of trouble with that in the beginning.

When Autumn started riding, she really gave us a hard time. I think I did pretty good at staying nice and positive, but when Cindy said to try to rephrase things, I realized I had a problem. I just kept saying the same thing over and over again! I'm going to work on it, though. It stinks that we're going to start going once every other week though. *Dramatic Sigh* It's not even that cold yet!

Kristie's story was sad. I think she's right about how blessed we all are. I don't think we appreciate everything quite as much as we should. Ever since my grandma died and my mom, I've began to appreciate the things I have a lot more. I've learned that they won't always be there.

* * *

At times the EAL activities can be difficult or frustrating. However, the goal for the activity is not always about completion but rather about performing to the best of your ability and learning from the overall process. Sometimes it takes the students several weeks to realize they have not failed if the task was not completed. Sometimes more can be learned from a truly challenging activity that the group was unable to complete. The purpose of EAL is learning life skills for teamwork, communication, and leadership, and at times the activities have less to do with the horses and more to do with the group than the students realize. Oftentimes when presented with difficult situations, students learn about what does not work, which in itself can be extremely useful. This particular week Cora was learning this lesson.

December 17, 2009

> Today was frustrating, but still totally worth it. Lunch was amazing, and I got to try frosted grapes for the first time. I didn't think I would like them [the horses], but they're actually not bad. The EAL activities were really frustrating, though. We couldn't talk or touch them, so leading them over hurdles was impossible. I tried everything I could to no avail. I'll be really interested when Cindy does it … The second activity was way more frustrating because I didn't understand, and I had to sit out even though other people were talking too. Today I learned that teamwork really does work best because you have different perspectives and ideas working together. I liked it!

* * *

Bonding with the horses is such a special part of Reaching for the Reins. It does not take long before each student develops a special bond with a particular horse. Cora's heart was big enough for two. She very quickly fell in love with both Pink Maggie and Nate.

January 14, 2010

> Today was fun! We all got to eat lunch together in Cindy's basement. I didn't have a sandwich in mine, but Nichole gave me her Fritos, so I didn't mind. Then we started grooming and saddling. I groomed Maggie, while Greg did her hooves. Then he and I worked together to saddle her up … Then we went into the arena to do EAL. The EAL was easier than usual, but still challenging. Greg and I messed up both time, but I think we might've gotten it right if we had tried again. Oh, well. So then we groomed Nate. I got to ride him! I love Nate! He's such a good horse! He's big, but he's so sweet. And he always gives me horse kisses.

* * *

During the cold winter months the students spend some of their time in Cindy's basement making woodworking projects to be used around the farm or merely as crafts. One of the students' favorite crafts is the exploding outhouse. The front of the small wooden box reads, "Hillbilly pay toilet, deposit 5¢ to open door." When a coin is dropped in the top, it triggers a mousetrap that makes the whole box explode. Not only do the students like creating them, even more they enjoy seeing someone get startled when one explodes.

February 10, 2010

Today was really fun! I've been asking to be able to go faster in the horses for so long, and now we can! I am amped about it! I totally can't stop smiling! We only got to trot a little, and it was really controlled, but it was still so much fun! It was the first time I'd ever ridden Lightning, and at first, his name intimidated me. But Autumn told me he was nice, so I relaxed. Nobody at the farm would let me do anything that would hurt me. I had a lot of fun riding Lightning. Martin got a workout jogging alongside of us. Lightning is said to have a preference for girls, but he seemed to get along with Martin quite well. I had fun building the exploding outhouses, too. I can't wait to give mine to my grandfather. He's gonna be so freaked out! Teehee! I can't wait until we get to trot again!

* * *

Some weeks, students leave the farm feeling discouraged, but the environment at the farm is so genuine and safe that they are always ready to give it another shot and start over the following week, ready and open to whatever the experience has to offer.

February 18, 2010

Today was great! We all ate lunch, then we (my group) got to go to the barn to get ready to ride. I think I did really bad. I couldn't remember how to do anything, or any names. I'm worried that I didn't learn as much as I was supposed to ... When we groomed, I remembered the curry, but I couldn't remember anything else. And when we saddled ... good grief. I was embarrassed. I'm working on it though ... At least I finished my exploding outhouse, though! I'm really excited to show it to my grandfather! TeeHee! It will be so funny. I'm so glad we started a fund from Reaching for the Rein to Cindy. It made her really happy! I wonder who they will donate to?

* * *

The first week of working with the Lighthouse students at the farm is full of unknowns. The Cedar Lane students are generally nervous about what to expect from their students and whether or not they are prepared enough to be responsible for another person. It is a huge shift of responsibility, and they generally feel a few butterflies.

March 2, 2010

Working with the kids today went much better than I thought it would. I had Gavin, and he was a really cool kid. He was very well behaved, and already knew most of what we tried to teach him. He was nice, too. I don't think he has anything he needs to improve on. I had a lot of fun working with Gavin!

March 18, 2010

Today, Sarah, Derek and I were in a group. We groomed and tacked the horse with Gavin, then took Josie outside to be ridden. Gavin liked riding, and did really well. When we were done riding we all went in the barn to clean saddles. It was fun, but Gavin was a little mischievous when he started towel snapping Derek. But in Gavin's defense, Derek started it. Then we raked hay outside. I think we helped Gavin to be more interested and active. Overall, I think Gavin is a great kid.

* * *

One of the main things Reaching for the Reins teaches the Cedar Lane students is to see the good in others and to help facilitate their growth in positive ways. We encourage the students to point out to their Lighthouse partners the things they do well and areas where they have seen them grow. Cora's positive outlook on life helped her encourage her students and helped them make the most of their experiences at the farm.

March 25, 2010

> Today was fun. I was in a group with Ava and Dayle. Dayle was a really great kid to work with. He was really well behaved, and listened. We took down snow fence, and put up electric fence. Then, Ava and I took Dayle riding. We did really well, even when we took him back to groom and untack. I think the thing I liked most today was riding. I didn't get to ride, but it was fun to work with Dayle around the arena and pep him up. Today, I learned that I've been brushing horses with the curry all the time. At least I have it right now.

* * *

Every year the students write a very difficult journal. Many of them have never had a safe venue to open up about the trials in their life, and writing it can be easier than telling someone, as they control how little or how much they'll write, without having to deal with any questions. One of the prompts I use is for them to write about the most difficult thing that has happened to them and how they got through it. When they've finished, I instruct them to fold the pages of their journal over and write the names on the outside of who they'll permit to read it. I make it clear they're able to designate anyone they choose—or no one at all. Whatever their wishes, it is important they feel they have complete control over their own stories and their own lives. Cora's difficult road is a testament to her resilience.

April 15, 2010

> One of the biggest impacts in my life would be my grandmother. My mother lost custody of me when I was two months old, and she was deemed an unfit parent. My grandmother fought to be granted guardianship and succeeded. My grandmother took care of me and she was always there for me, no matter what. She was, in essence, my mom. I love her very much. When I was eleven, her health started to deteriorate. By the time I was twelve, I found myself skipping school to take care of her. I took care of her for years. I did the best I could but it never seemed like enough. When I was fifteen, she was completely dependent on me. I had to feed her, bath her, and help her to the commode. I didn't like it but I loved her. None of the doctors knew what was wrong with her. She began having to make regular trips to the hospital. Finally, on December 27, 2007, at around 8:00 a.m., I got a phone call telling me that she had taken a turn for the worse and that was all I heard. My neighbor raced me to the hospital. By the time I got to the elevator, my grandfather was there with the news. She was gone. I went up to the room. Spent some time with her, and left. I miss her. You really don't know what you've got until it's gone.

Cora's grandmother died her freshman year. She expressed to me once how she felt guilty about those last few years with her grandmother.

She was frustrated at not being able to go to school or hang out with her friends, and now that her grandmother is gone, she feels guilty about having felt that frustration. She wishes that she had used that time to embrace the last few years with her and that she had more positive memories of her grandmother's last days.

When she received a call from the hospital telling her that her grandmother only had weeks to live, she called her mom, who came up from Arizona for the last few days of her grandmother's life and the funeral. This was the first time she had ever met her mother, and it was not a positive experience. Cora remembers having to call the police to come and remove her mother from her grandparents' home after the funeral because she was so drunk. The last gift she received from her mother was two sticks of lip gloss and a bottle of alcohol she had stolen from a local convenience store and dropped off for Cora on her way back to Arizona.

Cora's mom passed away in the spring of her senior year. When she came to school the next day, she was ready to open up about it. She told me she had never had a relationship with her mother and was sad to know they never would. When she was growing up, she received occasional letters from her mom from prison, and after her mother was paroled, Cora spoke to her once or twice on the phone.

While interviewing Cora for this book, she expressed her gratitude to the teachers at Cedar Lane for being sensitive and supportive of her during this time. Reflecting back on it, she said that her mom passing away didn't affect her nearly as much as her grandmother's passing, but she knew that the teachers cared for her and wanted to help her. She also expressed regret in that she wished her previous school had extended to her the empathy she'd found at Cedar Lane when her grandmother passed.

Cora only has one picture of her father. It is a picture of him holding her when she was a baby. A few years back, she tracked down his number and worked up the courage to call him, expressing an interest in meeting. From their conversation he seemed disinclined to meet her, so she resolved not to have a relationship with him and has not bothered to keep track of his whereabouts or contact information.

Shortly after her mother's death, Cora's grandfather, caretaker, and the only family she had left had a stroke. Even through this difficult time she remained focused on her schoolwork and was extremely dedicated to Reaching for the Reins. She knew that the Lighthouse students were counting on her, and she made it a priority to be at the farm to work with and teach them.

April 29, 2010

> Today was really fun. I was in a group with Haley (Yay!) and Bruce. We groomed Moe, then got Bruce up and ready to ride. He had fun, which was good. After working, we all got ice cream. It was yummy. I had fun, but it would've been easier if the kids hadn't all harassed me! RAWR! But, all in all, I would definitely come back for alumni day next year. That would be loads of fun. I love Reaching for the Reins, and I am really glad I signed up at the beginning of the year.

Cora's response to "What Reaching for the Reins Means to Me":

> Working at the farm really means a lot to me. For me Reaching for the Reins means working hard and working together like a family.

Reaching for the Reins has been an amazing experience. We've all created memories I'm sure we'll never forget!!

Epilogue

Reading and responding to student journals is how I generally learn about my students' lives. After several months of getting to know them they usually open up, which sheds new light on some of my previous interactions with them. When I look back through the experiences I have with them, some of the atypical things they say and some of the ways in which they express themselves become clear. I find the more time I spend with them, the more context I build, which is like trying to see through a clouded window one small scratch at a time. But with Cora I am continually awestruck at her insight and astounding resilience. She was only eighteen when we first met, and already she had lived through major surgery and pain, the abandonment and death of her mother, the death of her grandmother, and the imminent realization that the one person she has left, her grandfather, may soon be gone. And yet, for everything she has been through, she is to me the embodiment of joy.

Cora scored incredibly well on the ACT and is attending a local community college, where she is working on her associate's degree. She has not yet settled on what she wants to do for her four-year degree, but she realizes the sky is the limit and is unwilling to settle on any one thing yet. The summer after her graduation, she married her high school sweetheart. Cora, with her incredible resilience and unrestrained zest for life, has both the drive and motivation to be one of Cedar Lane's shining stars of success.

Chapter 17

Climbing Life's Ladders

The activities at the farm are designed to tap into the students' learning on many different levels. Some activities tie into the students' academic learning, while others teach them how to work in groups. These are the real-life surface skills that will help them further their academics or excel in the workforce. But there are also other activities that are crafted to generate deeper individual growth, activities designed to help students understand their pasts and equip them to be successful in their future endeavors. One of these personal growth activities is building life ladders. The first year, we started the project in a way that encouraged the students to embrace their vulnerabilities. Wally, one of the farm volunteers, shared his story and its life lessons to encourage the students to reflect and learn from their own journeys.

Wally's Story

Wally was a self-proclaimed adventuresome lad. A thrill seeker from the very beginning, flying planes became his passion. He soloed his first flight before graduating from high school and joined the air force to pursue his passion at nineteen. During his time in the air force he worked on airborne radios and radar for large cargo planes carrying supplies to Vietnam.

Not a whole lot changed when he met his wife and started a family at the age of twenty-nine. He spent much of his free time continuing his adventurous lifestyle. Risk taking aside, Wally greatly enjoyed working with his hands, pursuing woodworking, snowmobiling, and canoeing in addition to his passion for flying airplanes. When he was thirty-five, he discovered a lump in his tricep in the upper right arm. After consulting several physicians and undergoing surgical biopsies, he was diagnosed with a rare form of cancer. His initial treatment included daily chemotherapy with three different chemicals that lasted a week per month. His treatment as a whole lasted for over a year. After undergoing the treatment he was declared to be free of cancer. Five years after the initial diagnosis, the cancer returned in the same spot. His new treatment regimen used experimental chemotherapy and radiation. He was hospitalized for the entire treatment series and once again believed he'd beaten it. A year later the cancer returned again, requiring additional surgery and more experimental therapy. Wally remembers spending endless weeks over the period of several years at home in bed extremely ill as his family cared for him.

One afternoon when he was feeling good enough to get around a bit, he decided to change the oil in the car. While he was lying under the car, he attempted to extend his right arm to hold something. Instead of functioning as it should, it fell right back onto his chest. Wally was right-handed, but the repeated surgeries that eventually removed his tricep had left his arm unable to extend.

A year and a half later the cancer returned a fourth time. Facing down his options once again, Wally decided the only guaranteed treatment was amputation, which included the entire right arm and shoulder.

Wally does not begrudge his experience. Instead, he tries to look at the positive things that have come out of the course of his life. He realizes that his adventurous lifestyle kept him away from his children and could have taken his life years ago. Wally is quick to acknowledge that those long hours recovering from treatments produced a changed mind-set and created a wonderful bond between him and his family. Even though the cancer consumed his life for over ten years, rather than allowing it to define him, he chose to use it to shape him into a better person.

* * *

Wally wrapped up his talk by revealing a handmade six-car wooden train. The cars were solid cherry with a black walnut boiler and maple wheels. Every detail of the cars was carefully thought-out, from the engine's perfectly sculpted smokestack to the loader car, complete with a swiveling crane and crank. It was evident that many hours of precision craftsmanship had gone into each feature. Wally has made forty-three trains in his life, nine before he lost his arm and thirty-four after. He has not allowed the loss of his right arm to stop him from doing the things he found joy in. Instead, it inspired his ingenuity, causing him to figure out ways of using clamps and other devices to hold things in place so that even with one arm he can turn rough lumber into beautifully crafted masterpieces. His intent in sharing his story was to inspire the students to understand that regardless of the experiences that shaped them, they are still able to set their goals high and accomplish anything they set their minds to.

Wally's challenge to the students was for them to think about their lives and to make miniature ladders that represented where they have been and what their goals are for the future. Every part of the ladder was to tell the story of their lives, whether uplifting or heartbreaking.

The students were provided with wood, nails, glue, wire, paint, and a plethora of other building materials. Over the years we've noted how different students approach this task. Some students are intimidated by the task and quietly ponder their approach. Others seem to find their destiny in launching headfirst into the task. Regardless of their approach, the students' creativity is immediately evident. Some of them represent a specific time in their lives with each rung of their ladder. Rungs were broken, missing, crooked, or bound together in the middle with wire, each unique feature symbolic to a specific memory or experience in their lives. A few paint their ladders in different colors to represent their circumstances. Others use pipe cleaners to make little stick figures climbing the ladder to show where they are in their journeys. The amount of thought and creativity the students pour into the activity is always inspiring.

* * *

The day Wally told his story was one of the most poignant moments in the program for Cal because of how it impacted Jeremy. In response to Wally's story, Jeremy opened up to share his story with Cal. As Cal was walking around helping students and talking to them about their creations, one student's ladder caught his attention. Cal noticed that Jeremy's ladder had a lot of nails. Some of the nails were obviously holding pieces together, but others appeared not to have a purpose and were not driven all of the way into the wood. Cal was naturally curious, but he also didn't want to pry too much into the young man's private life. As he passed, he casually asked what the nails signified in such a way that it encouraged Jeremy to share as much or as little as he was comfortable with. Jeremy didn't even look up from his work as he replied with a smile, "You'll see." Cal accepted the answer and resumed his circling of the room, looking for others who might need a hand. As the afternoon progressed, Jeremy found his way back to Cal with his completed ladder. Cal saw that he added several more nails in various places on his ladder and wove wire around them to create several different configurations. One was a heart while another, the one Cal saw him creating, looked like bars. Jeremy explained that each of the figures represented a time in his life, which included heartbreak, tragedy, love, and even jail. The young man's artistic nature had really flourished in his creation, and it seemed as though the process had been as introspective and cathartic for him as it was refreshing for Cal. He eagerly shared with Cal how he was now looking toward graduation and a brighter future full of meaning.

On the ride back to school, the students were prompted to write about their ladders in their journals. While some of their words are a bit choppy, they truly capture the meaning they crafted into their handiwork and how difficult some of their lives have been. Their courage, honesty, and willingness to share their vulnerability is astounding.

January 20, 2011

Derek

It's been a month since I was at Reaching for the Reins. Well today we all had 2 lunches then brushed the horses and put the saddle over it and what not. Then we went down to the basement and was building a ladder or railroad tracks out of sticks. The physical appearance of the sticks symbolizes the meaning in one's life. Mine Symbolizes from birth and then mutual feels and then reached a point where the cuts symbolized the scars mentally the upward spiral represents I'm learning gradually my mind is getting older more aware of my surroundings which on the side of it are scars and nails upward meaning pain and anger but I'm getting stronger about it. So today was a great day but also expressing our past, present and future lives.

Jason

The rungs on my ladder represent past relationships, hardships and the people in my life. I put a ladder rung on both sides of the ladder to represent how each story has 2 sides.

Ally

My ladder was based on the positives and negatives in my life. Whether it was a family member dying or something that happened a while ago ... I think that making my ladder showed me and made me realize that everything I've been through make me the person I am today.

Sarah

My ladder goes by my sixteen years of my life. It starts bad, when I was 1½ years old I had a breathing problem and doctors said I had an ear infection but I did not, and that's why it starts with wire holding it together to show that I was really close to dying. My thirteen year was when I had surgery for my gallbladder. I had gallstones it really did hurt when they took it out but now I still have the pain, don't know why though. Also I'm glad I'm back.

Greg

The steps on my ladder are times I fell and mistakes that I made and had to fix. And the last step I didn't finish because I'm not done climbing.

Samantha

My ladder is bumpy but got better. A couple of my pieces stand for when my father left when I was born. Mostly how he treats me.

Phil

Today we made ladders that represent times in our lives. One of the rungs on it is broke because that represents when my Uncle died. I was named after him. We have the same first, middle, and last name. I was close to him when he was still alive. Now I do what I can to think positive about it.

Ray

Well my ladder is about my life and everything that has happened in my life. About how I don't remember anything from five to thirteen, and I don't know why. But I'm happy that I don't remember because the things I do remember I really don't like. I wish I didn't remember. I understand what this ladder is talking about. How things in your life happen to you. You have to put them behind you and look for something better and that there are better things out there. My life is one of those lives. I always look for the better things in life. I don't let the things that happen to me put me down and I always think about my choices and my life and the ones that I make and I make sure that they are positive choices.

Chapter 18

Growing Together

Cohesion among a group of young adults is almost impossible. Each has his or her own personality, ideas, and priorities. This makes it extremely difficult for them to work together as a team, and at times the tension is so negative that differing opinions can escalate into irreconcilable disagreements or fights. Building relationships where they learn to work together is an important part of Reaching for the Reins.

The first few weeks we attend the farm there are always defined social groups. Each week different groups are assigned so students have the opportunity to work with different individuals to help them build relationships outside their normal social sphere. This is an integral part of the program, as it exposes normally exclusive groups to others they would not interact with under normal circumstances. As the groups are switched from week to week and students work with more and more of their peers, the disparities between them begin to blur. It is rare that all of the students get along all the time, but generally a healthy respect for the other students' personalities and opinions forms as they spend time interacting and sharing experiences together.

One memorable year, after about six weeks of the program the group still had not started to form bonds. There were still clearly defined clique structures among the groups. Several of the students were actively asking to be placed in certain groups because they wanted to avoid specific students with differing personalities. The volunteers and I noticed the lack of cooperation and knew that in order to best serve our Lighthouse students, who would join the program in just a few short weeks, the students needed to integrate and develop a team mentality. We were ready for the challenge.

* * *

The EAL activity the following week centered around obstacles. In the center of the arena, Autumn, one of our volunteers, created an elaborate maze of ground poles, ropes, and cones. Throughout the maze she scattered all sorts of wonderful temptations: a small pile of hay on a chair, a handful of grain in a pan on top of a barrel, and a few treats placed at random. The goal was to give the horses some areas throughout the maze where they might get stuck on an obstacle.

Students were paired in twos with a horse. Each student was given a ten-foot lead rope with the horse situated between them. The students were only permitted to hold on to the very end of the rope, and together they were to guide the horse through the maze.

The first few groups of students attempted the task with little success. As they started the horse through the maze, the strategically placed distractions complicated the students' efforts. As each horse passed a temptation, it stopped at each to munch its fill before proceeding on to the next morsel. One student would tug on one side and the other student on the other side to no avail. The students were not communicating with each other and pulled the horse in opposite directions. With a lack of clear signals, the horse chose to do as it wished. Many of their classmates who were looking on were disengaged.

Que was definitely the worst. The fifteen-hand buckskin has a tendency to do as he pleases. His round belly is evidence enough that his mind is always focused on food. Que, true to his nature, became hung up in the bucket of grain, and Ray and Phil could not get his greedy nose out of it. They coaxed and gently tugged this way and that, but he refused to budge. Minutes went by, and the grain in the bucket disappeared. Many of the onlookers showed signs of boredom and annoyance. Finally, only when he had eaten every bit, Que moved on of his own accord, and the teens were able to maneuver him out of the maze.

After witnessing the boys' battle with Que and observing several other groups struggle their way through, Jeremy and Kathy decided to take a different approach. They started to talk to each other as they went along. They pointed out possible pitfalls that the horse might become distracted by to each other and worked together to gently guide the horse around the appealing treats. As they progressed quickly through the maze the rest of the group started to perk up. When they exited, several of their classmates congratulated them on their success. As the next group started to enter the maze, the group of onlookers began to coach and encourage them through. When a horse became hung up on one of the temptations, the rest of the group would yell out suggestions on how their classmates could maneuver the horse away from the sticky spot.

By the end of the activity the students had opened up to each other in an entirely new way. While processing the completed activity as a group, they talked about successes that each group had experienced and about how working together made a task that started out difficult much easier in the end. They also talked about obstacles in their own lives and how having support can help you through tough times.

From that point on the group of teens was much different. While they didn't get along all of the time, they had experienced the success that comes with working together as a team, and they managed to harness this spirit as they moved forward with the program. They began to laugh and joke together and look at mistakes as opportunities to learn with each other.

Every year since, I have looked for the moment in the program where I see this shift. Most years the shift is subtler than it was this particular year, but there is always a moment that hits me when I know the group has finally found cohesion. As adults, the volunteers and I always like to look back at progress and what moves students forward. Who would have thought that this year the catalyst was temptation?

* * *

January 14, 2010

Ava

The EAL was easier. It was nice to be able to talk but really didn't at first. Then we gave each other advice and encouragement.

Nichole

I really liked the activity we did with obstacles. Life has so many obstacles to go through. Some are very hard to go through. But you have to believe in and inspire yourself and push yourself. That was my favorite EAL.

Eric

I liked the EAL today. It signified obstacles. And I know a lot about obstacles in life. Except in the EAL I had someone to help me through them.

Greg

It was awesome today. The EAL was one of the easiest we've had. This time we had more to work with. Two people had to hold the end of the rope. Two ropes on each side. We had to lead the horse through the alley of temptation. They couldn't give in to any temptation or knock over any obstacles. We got it done though. It was like it was real life. When we come across a temptation not to give in. Sometimes you have someone older to lead you to success.

Haley

I liked the activity we did today. It helped me look at my obstacles in life in a new way. I have had a very rough life and have many many obstacles I'm still facing lots of obstacles that I was also facing as a child. But now I see that it may take a couple of times to get through an obstacle but if you stay strong and keep trying you'll get through it.

Chapter 19

The Gathering Place

Cal's cabin has become the official unofficial Reaching for the Reins gathering place during the summer. Using his years of construction experience, Cal built a small log cabin from fallen trees in a remote, shaded corner of his property. The cabin is tucked away on a slight hill in the woods and overlooks a small clearing with a fire pit. The structure of the cabin is perfect for country gatherings and has hosted many Reaching for the Reins summer events. The main floor has a long, handcrafted log table surrounded by rough-hewn benches, while on the opposite side of the cabin sits a wrought-iron cooking and heating stove and several handcrafted cabinets. Above the kitchen area is a cozy loft with a wood frame bed. All of the fixtures and features are handcrafted from reclaimed wood Cal found around his property. One of his specialties is constructing lamps with bases made from gnarled pieces of wood that exhibit a certain eye-catching character. Every summer all of the students and volunteers gather there because we can't wait until fall to see each other again. The cabin is a perfect little getaway to hang out and share food, stories, and fun.

During one summer get-together, Phil and Evan fell in love with the cabin. Wanting to spend more time in its quiet setting, they shyly approached Cal to see if he would agree to them spending a night or two in the cabin sometime. He enthusiastically agreed, and the boys quickly planned their adventure. Although their first stay went well, they had to pack up early, as they had underestimated just how much food they could go through in such a short amount of time. However, they determined that the following summer they would return for another cabin stay.

Learning from their previous stay, the boys spent a year dreaming, planning, and saving for their second adventure. They planned to spend Phil's birthday weekend at the cabin and had saved the money they made from helping Cindy with hay to buy food and other provisions. When the weekend finally came, they were confident of their preparation and were extremely excited.

As they drove onto Cal's farm Friday afternoon, they checked in with him and began their weekend adventure. Cal's property has all the things teenage boys could ever hope for. It comes complete with open fields, woods for exploring, and a well-stocked pond for fishing. The boys made their way through the fields back to the cabin, set up their stuff, and started a fire. Cal didn't hear a peep out of the boys until Saturday night, when he and his wife Sue received a phone call. The boys were calling to invite them out to the cabin for supper to thank them for letting them stay in the cabin for the weekend. They also called Cindy to invite her out.

When Cal, Sue, and Cindy arrived, they found the boys with hot dogs, buns, and an already roaring fire. As they shared the meal together, the boys told them of their adventures and how they had been planning and saving for this weekend for a whole year. The boys had planned from the very beginning of their trip to have extra food for Saturday night so they could share it with Cal, Sue, and Cindy. The boys' three guests were impressed by how responsible the boys were and how thoughtful it was of them to have invited them to dinner.

Cal and Sue left the cabin that night with promises to come out and cook the boys breakfast early the next morning. They assured the boys that they would wake up to the smell of pancakes cooking on the wrought-iron woodstove. However, when Cal and Sue arrived the next morning, the boys were not only up, but they had gotten up quite early to prepare the cabin. Cal and Sue marveled at how neat and tidy the place was and how the boys had swept out both the cabin and the porches. The responsibility they exhibited and the obvious attention taken in caring for the cabin made both Cal and Sue proud of them.

Before the boys left, they acknowledged having admired the lamps in the cabin and indicated an interest in making a lamp. So Cal sent them on a quest to hunt around the woods and find some unique pieces of wood. An hour or so later they showed up at his workshop with two interesting hunks of wood. Even though they would not have enough time to complete the project, the trio set to work on starting the lamps. First, they would have to drill a hole through the center of the logs so that they could install a piece of conduit to run the electric cords through. Then, once the light socket was mounted and the lamp wired, they would have to finish the wood with varnish and top it with a lampshade.

Evan's piece came complete with a little smear of bird poop down the side. Of course, Cal and the boys' imaginations started to run wild. They decided that the poop would have to stay on the log and that they would build the lamp in such a way to include this natural feature. Even though they did not have time to execute the plan, it was decided that they would get a fake bird from the craft store and mount it above the poop. They would then varnish the nugget right into the work of art so that it would be a permanent part of their handiwork. The plan made all three smile, and when the boys had to leave partway through the wiring process, they agreed to return soon to finish off the project.

Cal is looking forward to the boys spending more time at the cabin and finishing up their lamp projects. He never dreamed that his serene little hideaway in the woods would become so special for so many different people. Having the boys come out and spend some time in the cabin gave them all a chance to get to know each other a little better. Cal enjoyed teaching the boys how to start the process of wiring the lamps and was impressed with their generosity in having Sue, Cindy, and himself out for dinner. These are the stories that make giving back so meaningful.

Chapter 20

Through Sarah's Eyes

Have you ever felt overlooked, unimportant, and insignificant, as if those around you don't notice you or care about what you have to say? Have you ever felt as if no one would miss you if you were gone? It's a lonely existence from this perspective. You second-guess everything you say and do because you're worried about what others will think, and, eventually, you learn to avoid saying anything at all for fear of others' reactions. Sarah's story starts out from this introverted world of self-seclusion and can be best told through her memories and feelings. For this reason I have chosen to tell Sarah's story differently from the others.

Sarah's story is told in the first person to provide a glimpse from her perspective. Her story could not be told in this manner were it not for her unique insights and express permission. To capture her insights I had several extensive and candid conversations with her prior to piecing this story together. To remain true to Sarah's vision, and because this story is told in Sarah's voice, Sarah was given full editing license over the completed story. The following story is wholly Sarah's.

* * *

Everyone saw me as shy. I hate that word. I am not even sure exactly what it means. Sure, I don't talk around people, and if given the chance, I shrink into the corner. But I'm not shy. I have something to say, and I want to be heard. I want to be a part of whatever is going on just like everyone else. I just ... don't.

I've never had many friends. I usually just hang out with my mom's friends' kids or a couple of girls on my street. But even then I don't really talk to them. Not much, anyway. We all just hang out, and I sit in the corner and listen to them talk. Sometimes I speak up, but my voice comes out so quiet.

I grew up with my mom and her second husband, but I have her first husband's last name even though he's not my dad. My mom is the one who has always taken care of me. I remember when I was little I would see my dad on Christmas. He and his parents would come over and give me presents. But that stopped about ten years ago. My grandparents had a new grandchild, and they forgot about me. My dad doesn't even remember me most of the time. I don't like the way that makes me feel. I just feel like I'm really unimportant to him.

I spent my academic career in the same school system and saw the same students and teachers each day, but I never got very comfortable with them. I just sat quietly back and listened. It's funny how much you can learn about people and circumstances if you pay attention. I always knew the latest gossip of who was dating or being cheated on. I didn't really care about it; I just knew because I listened.

I wouldn't say I am a great student, but I am not terrible either. I mostly got Cs, a few Bs from time to time. School was just blah. My biggest problem with school is that I don't understand so much of what the teachers are explaining, and I never ask questions. I remember one math teacher who used to explain things so fast and give you five different ways to solve a problem, and all that did was confuse me. I would start the problem using one of her methods and then switch halfway through. I wish she had just made it simple.

By the time I got to high school I was living with my mom, her fiancé, her ex-husband, and her brother in a two-bedroom house we had been renting for a couple of years. Times are tough, and my mom has a hard time keeping a job, so we did what we had to to get by. The house is crowded, though, and it's hard to live and make accommodations for everyone else's personalities and bad habits.

The start of my freshman year was pure chaos. The hallways always seemed overcrowded during passing periods. The amount of people just bothered me. The teachers always seemed busy and off task, and they were never available for one-on-one help. I only lasted three weeks. I had to get out of there.

That's when I came to Cedar Lane. I like how small it is. I knew a few students who were going to school here. One girl, Cora, lived on my street, and we hung out sometimes. Cedar Lane was different than a regular high school. The teachers and staff showed they cared. They talked to me one-on-one. At first it was kind of weird. I had never had a teacher come up to me and ask questions, let alone care about the answers. I liked it though. I liked interacting. It made me feel important.

I joined Reaching for the Reins because I wanted to make friends. I wanted to be a part of something. I wasn't sure how I was going to do it, but I wanted to try.

My first week at the farm I was nervous. I had no idea what to expect, and I'd never touched a horse before. They are so big. I guess I knew they were big, but when you stand right next to them they seem even bigger. And I didn't realize how much they would smell. Well, it's really their poo that smells. Luckily, Cora was in the program with me, so that gave me a bit of a security blanket. She is such an upbeat and outgoing person, which helps me when I am in situations where I feel uncomfortable.

It's amazing how much I learned each week at the farm. From the first day we just dove right in. I learned about barn chores and maintenance. It was kind of fun learning how to use some of the tools. Then, during the EAL activities, we found out how horses communicate through body language. I was intrigued by how good their relationships are with each other and how they respect each other and how they can have that same level of respect with people if we learn to read their body language. I learned that one of the most important things is to stay calm when you are working with the horse because they're constantly reading your body language. If you're tense or hyper, they will be too.

One of my favorite memories at the farm was a few weeks into the program. That's when I rode a horse for the first time. I remember that I was scared. I knew Nate wasn't going to do anything wild because he was so good when I was brushing and saddling him. It's amazing how you can build a relationship of trust simply through grooming the horses. Grooming is so calming and relaxing, especially when you know the horse enjoys it too. And all of them have such unique personalities. Nate likes jellybeans. When I took him into the arena and walked him around, I was really nervous, but Pat, his owner, and everyone else in the arena, encouraged me. So I just got up there and did it. It's funny how things change, because riding used to be a fear, but now it is relaxing.

Another memory that sticks out in my mind involves my dad. Most of the time he doesn't even remember me but this day he actually called my mom and me, and I went over to his house. He was drunk when we got there, but he did speak to me a bit and seemed to know who I was.

Here is how it happened: about halfway through the program we met the Lighthouse boys for the first time at the Silver Beach Carousel. One of the horses in the carousel is a special needs rider's horse. Since Reaching for the Reins is all about working with horses and helping others, we all met there and rode the carousel, hung out in the Discovery Zone, and had pizza. I was apprehensive to meet the boys for the first time. They had so much energy running around the Discovery Zone. They wore me out. My student's name was Carl. He had the biggest smile. I worked in a group with Cora and Greg. I let them do most of the talking. I interacted with him some, but it was kind of intimidating. It was our job to get to know him and start teaching him how to have healthy relationships and communicate in groups. That was kind of hard for me because I still struggled with that myself. Cora and Greg did great with him though, and I learned from them.

Two news stations showed up with cameras that day and also a couple of newspaper reporters. Mrs. Carlsen is always running around with cameras, and I hate it. I always look annoyed in pictures, probably because I hate having my picture taken. They interviewed several people, and that night my dad saw me on the news. That's when he called, and my mom and I went over. Even though he was kind of out of it, I guess it felt good to know that deep down he still knows who I am.

My second year at Cedar Lane I started out in Reaching for the Reins, but I started to have a lot of medical issues. My stomach was bothering me, and the doctor figured out it was my gallbladder. I had to have it removed. It hurt so badly, and I missed a ton of school.

The weird thing is, though, that it still hurts off and on. Sometimes I still miss school for several days at a time because of my stomach. I have gone to the doctor several times since the surgery, but nothing seems to work. They tried giving me painkillers, but they just make me upset to my stomach so I don't take them. I usually just hang out at home in my room in pain for days. I kind of start to feel depressed sometimes when my stomach is bothering me. Because of my medical problems, I missed several weeks of school and was dropped from the Reaching for the Reins. I was really upset about it because I really loved the program the first year and was so proud of myself for everything I accomplished. I learned so much about life and myself.

Now in my third year at Cedar Lane, I am back in Reaching for the Reins and doing great. I have had a few really cool experiences this year, and I keep learning new things. One thing I learned was to never judge a book by its cover. I think one of the reasons I don't talk much is because there are certain people who I have decided I just won't get along with or who I just don't care to get to know. One week I was put in a group with Mandy. I always thought she was a preppy girly girl and that I wouldn't be able to work with her. But after spending a couple of minutes with her I realized she is not that way at all. I had a good time working with her on saddling and grooming and got to know her pretty well. I am not sure we will ever really hang out, but it was cool to get to know her, and it really opened my eyes. I could be missing out on opportunities to meet new people and make new friends.

It's also kind of cool to have been in the program a year and a half already because I know a lot of things that I can use to help out my group. One of my coolest memories from this year was one of the EAL activities. We had to try to get the two horses that were in the arena into two pockets on the ground made out of boards.

Each group member was given thirty seconds to speak and be the leader of the group. During those thirty seconds, that person was completely in charge. When the thirty seconds were over, it was the next person's turn to talk and lead. I positioned myself at the end of the group and let several of my group members go first. Some of them didn't lead at all, and some had suggestions for trying to move the horses that didn't work at all. But I had done the EAL before. I don't think I had ever done it successfully, but I had tried it a previous year, and so this year I had an idea that I thought might work. When it came my turn to speak and lead the group, I actually stood up and told my classmates what to do. I confidently barked out orders to them, and they did what I told them to do. And the cool thing was it worked. We got the horses to go where we wanted them and finished the activity. It felt really good to stand up and take charge. I'd never done that before. Usually I'm content being a follower. But you know, I find myself letting my opinion out more with friends, too. It's kind of funny now, because sometimes I say things they don't want to hear. It's like now that I have started talking, I am honest when they ask my opinions, and sometimes they are not ready for what I have to say.

Being a leader this year with the Lighthouse boys has been so much fun. I feel like I am really good at it. I think before I was even scared to ask the teachers and volunteers for help, so I didn't want to teach anything because if I got stuck I wouldn't know what to do. But now I know I can just ask for help, so I am not nervous about trying. This year I am working with Ben. He is such a cool kid. I like to learn about what he likes to do and teach him about the horses. He learns so fast and seems to really enjoy spending time with the horses.

Reaching for the Reins has taught me so much these last three years and has actually impacted my life in a huge way. I was hoping to just make connections with people, but I find I got way more out of it than that. As I look back through the pictures of my time in Reaching for the Reins over the last three years, I look less and less annoyed. I am starting to smile, and I don't shy away as much. In fact, to tell you the truth, I don't really mind my picture being taken.

I also like that I have found my voice. I used to struggle so much in school and personally because I never asked for help. Now I know that if I ask, there are people out there who will help. That has changed my life so much. My old friendships are even growing because of it. I talk a lot more to my friends, and, because of that, we hang out a lot more. I like being a part of the group and feeling like I am genuinely involved instead of sitting back observing.

* * *

Sarah is a completely different person than the one who first joined the program. Her involvement in the program has given her an immense amount of confidence; so much, in fact, that she surprises us from time to time with the extent of her newfound confidence. She smiles so much more now and interacts with a couple of our students who are a bit shy, trying to pull them out of their shell as well. Like many Cedar Lane students who blossom under the one-on-one attention and special programs like Reaching for the Reins, Sarah does not want to leave. Truth be told, I don't blame her. No matter where my career takes me, part of my heart will always be there too. Like Sarah participating in the program, facilitating the program has taught me a tremendous amount about my own life and helped me to experience it more fully.

Sarah's thoughts from her 2011–12 yearbook page

> Everyone in this program is like brothers and sisters we are so close. If we weren't in this program I probably wouldn't

of met any of these really amazing people. Reaching for the reins has completely changed my life in ways I didn't know was possible. If I weren't in this amazing program I would still be really shy. I am really outgoing now. I love to talk, can't stop talking. Have more friends then ever!!! And two very important best friends, because of Reaching for the Reins. My relations with everyone including my family have changed.

Love & Pride

My love for this program has grown. I take pride in everything I do now. I have never done anything this life changing. For now I will continue my life with my chin up high and have all the confident I could possibly have thanks to Reaching for the Reins.

Chapter 21

Wisdom's Struggle with Anger

Whenever Derek struggled to overcome a challenge, he would stalk around the school with a scowl on his face. He clung to this rough exterior as though it were sustaining him. When his frustration levels were at their highest, he would relentlessly pace back and forth, alternating between clenched fists or repeatedly pummeling his open palm with his fist. When confronted, he articulated his frustration in terms of people always working against him.

Derek's first week in Reaching for the Reins was the catalyst needed to change his attendance and grades and to start him on a path to interacting more with his peers. But his anger continued to hold him back. This pervasive negativity didn't go unnoticed by the volunteers at the farm. They quickly realized the year was his last in the program and that time was running out to help him work through his anger before he graduated. Joan and Cal decided they would try to engage Derek with a little extra time to see if they could crack his gruff exterior.

Late Bus

Late one afternoon while most of the students were finishing practice sessions teaching the volunteers how to saddle and ride the horses,

Derek and a few other students were working with Cal, constructing a set of steps for Cindy. The students enjoy making little things to say thank you to Cindy. Coupled with this is the opportunity to learn about and work with tools and, more importantly, with Cal. Perhaps the closest thing to a father figure many of them will have, he is a patient teacher and always manages to entertain in addition to instruct. Because of these qualities, the students enthusiastically anticipate their time with him, knowing they will come away with positive, fun memories of their time spent working together. Many of the students have a limited context in interacting positively with adults, so they are eager to work with and learn from the volunteers as often as possible. Much of what they learn from week to week is entirely new to them, and without the program they would likely have little opportunity to experience them.

To build the steps, Cal showed Derek how to operate the drill and change out the different bits so he could drill the pilot holes and turn in the screws. Within a half hour, the small group completed the steps and joined the rest of the group.

On a typical day when the work is complete, the students gather together and joke around while they wait for the bus. Usually, the bus arrives on schedule, so when a few minutes passed and it didn't show, we called to inquire about the holdup and learned the bus was running about a half hour late. This gave the students a little more downtime to hang out.

Since the Christmas party, the Reaching for the Reins students established Cindy's basement as the unofficial headquarters for operations at the farm. Rather than mill around with the rest of the students, Derek retreated to the basement to lounge on the love seat, everyone's favorite resting spot. That is where Joan ambushed him.

One of Joan's many strengths is asking questions and *expecting* responses, and she makes it difficult for someone to give her a vague answer. Having cornered him, she warmed him up by asking about school and his family, and then she pointed out that he seemed upset. When asked why, he gave his canned response that he felt people were working against him. She nodded understandingly and began to ask more pointed questions. He shared his frustration in being a fifth-year senior and that it was going to take him the whole year to graduate instead of the half year for which he was hoping. He described his frustration that he would be graduating at twenty instead of the typical graduation age of eighteen. Joan was quick to explain this wasn't something he should be frustrated with or embarrassed by. She shared that she did not think any teen was ready to go into the world at eighteen and that most kids take longer to mature, so even if they were done with school, they were not yet fully equipped to be successful. Joan encouraged Derek by pointing out the positive qualities that would help make him successful after graduation and that age was of little consequence.

Although these encounters may seem small and insignificant, it is interactions like these that I believe pushed Derek toward a more positive path. Ever since that day in the basement where he had the conversation with Joan, he seemed to be a bit easier on himself and those around him. The change was subtle, but there was evidence that her words helped the wheels to start turning.

Progression

The change in Derek's approach to life was not instantaneous. He still stewed from time to time, but it seemed his frustration began to occur less frequently and plagued him for shorter periods of time. Even when he was not necessarily angry, he often had a dour expression on his face.

One afternoon, Derek was looking through all the pictures taken during Reaching for the Reins while compiling his yearbook pages when he looked up and asked why he always looked angry in his pictures. I told him it was because he never smiled. He looked puzzled as I explained how he often looked unhappy. After a moment's pause he responded by saying that he'd never considered it before and that it was not exactly a reflection of how he felt, that even though he frequently appeared to be angry he was not necessarily upset all the time.

For several weeks after our conversation I made it a point to smile at him in an attempt to elicit a smile in return. Admittedly, this was a small challenge for me, as it runs against the grain to smile at someone insistent on an unhappy expression. At first he shook it off like I was crazy, but if Derek taught me anything it is that persistence pays big dividends. It took awhile, but his first smile made the effort worthwhile.

When I interviewed Derek for this book, he shared with me that his teenage years had been difficult, but that he'd made a conscious decision to be his own psychiatrist and work through his anger in more positive ways. Over time, he'd become more aware of how he expressed himself and how this affected his emotional equilibrium. He spent so much time trying to rationalize his frustrations that instead of finding an outlet he had allowed them to stagnate. And while his remedies to better his mood were to work out or hang out with friends, the extent of his frustration prevented him from ever fully letting go of his anger. Through this, he came to the realization that he had his whole life ahead of him and that he should make the most of it.

A Whole New Derek

The changes in Derek were so subtle to start with that I thought I was imagining them. However, my "Ahah!" moment with Derek came after one of the volunteers at the farm, Aimee, offered to take senior pictures for the seniors in Reaching for the Reins. As I drove the three students out to the farm one foggy morning, I experienced the full transformation Derek had made over the last two years.

As anyone who has ever ridden in a vehicle with a teen knows, they are incapable of riding in a car without the radio on. Personally, I am not an adherent to the genres of rap or hip-hop, so after a little negotiation, the students reluctantly settled on country. As the music played, Derek began to sing along with the most mocking country twang he could muster. And when he grew tired of this he regaled us with stories about his family and crazy brother. Most of his stories ended with funny punch lines, and, when he realized his knack for entertaining, he started in on redneck jokes. He had the whole car in stitches the entire ride.

When we reached the farm, I could not help but smile as the group piled out. Derek had made two distinct transformations in the last two years, transformations that would enable him to be more successful in every aspect of his life as he moved forward. Not only had he integrated into a structured environment and met clearly established goals, he was also able to let his guard down and interact with and build relationships with adults and peers. Derek is the embodiment of what Reaching for the Reins was created to accomplish: assisting students in becoming more personally, academically, and socially equipped for success.

My Wish

I am so proud of Derek and all of his peers. All of the Reaching for the Reins students over the past five years have overcome inconceivable difficulties and have used this opportunity to build momentum for their futures. I am proud of them for all they have accomplished both at school and at the farm. I have seen them grow into strong, capable, and talented individuals who have a life's worth of possibilities ahead of them. My wish for each of them is that they set their goals high and work hard toward success. When life gets hard, I hope they all remember to draw from their strengths and remember what they have already accomplished. They have a strong foundation and now they need to fly.

Chapter 22

To ... Fly

Nanci was a boarder at Circle "C" Stable when she heard about Reaching for the Reins. Cindy happened to mention it to her one day, and, as we were to learn was typical Nanci fashion, she jumped at the chance to become one of our volunteers. In love with the big city life, Nanci lives in the bustle and flow of Chicago's slipstream, but her soul rests an hour and a half away in a little corner of southwest Michigan with her horse. She describes horses as little doctors who see into and open up our hearts to healing. When her twenty-seven-year-old horse passed away, she immediately started to search for another one because she knew that having a horse in her life was vitally important.

Nanci has a special way of seeing the inner light in the students. As she worked with them from week to week that first year, she recognized their damaged pasts and saw the embers that still burned deep within them. The weeks she spent in the program progressed into months, and she witnessed (and aided) many of these embers to grow into flames that transformed the students.

Witnessing this transformation in the students also ignited a spark in Nanci. In keeping with her gregarious personality, Nanci spends her spare time as a singer/songwriter in a five-member band called Just Listen Band. Her contribution to the group is to write, arrange, and perform a variety of songs for a wide range of events. When she learned of the annual award ceremony at the end of the program in which the students are provided certificates of recognition for their hard work and dedication, she committed to write and sing a song in dedication to the program and in recognition of their efforts.

Nanci only had a month to pull off the venture, and the creation of the song became one of the toughest endeavors she has undertaken. It was vital to her to capture everything that Reaching for the Reins embodied. The transformation of lives, touching moments, and meaningful memories, as well as friendships and connections, all had to be woven into the thread in some way.

Over the course of that month, Nanci wrote and rewrote and re-rewrote the song seventeen times. Each time she finished, only to discover while driving to work or rehearsing with the band that it was not good enough yet, that she had missed an element or detail she could not afford to leave out. Over the course of its development, ideas and phrases were scribbled on scraps of paper and napkins and envelopes—anything she could get her hands on when inspiration struck—and pieced together time and time again.

When it was finally done, she said she had an amazing sense of peace, and only two days to get it recorded. One of her band members, John, wrote an incredible bass line to accompany her acoustic guitar and vocals. They recorded the song in their studio, Treehouse Studios, in Winthrop Harbor, Illinois. She rushed to get copies made in time for the debut performance.

* * *

All of the students gathered in the Circle "C" arena in a semicircle of folding chairs. While the students were spending their last few hours at the farm soaking in memories and friendships, Nanci and John had nonchalantly set up their sound equipment. As the group filed in and grew silent, Nanci announced her gift to the students.

When she started to sing, it only took a moment to realize that this was not an ordinary song. The fourth line gives it away by identifying Cedar Lane. As the students heard those words, they turned to each other in amazement. Their faces were beaming, and some had tears in their eyes.

As the song concluded, it was evident that they got the message. They were special. They had experienced the transformational journey that the song so eloquently conveys, and their hearts had been opened to the new possibilities that their lives now held. They were equipped with new tools for tackling life's challenges, and they were ready to go out into the world and share what they had learned.

The song is now used yearly in our program videos as well as promotional materials. I love seeing the faces of people who hear it for the first time, watching them as they are blown away by the fact that Reaching for the Reins is more than playing with ponies. It is about enhancing lives, broadening perspectives on what is possible, motivating people to be the best that they can be, and building self-esteem and courage that can overcome any challenge. It is about showing young and old lives alike that if the hoofbeats of our heart are beating together, the sky is the limit, and we can fly.

Reaching for the Reins Song
Composed by Nanci Launius
Copyright 2010
Used by permission.

Look at you
Shining Bright
You move the darkness to the light
And when you came from Cedar Lane
You helped us all grow together.
You've learned to be leaders … its true
And in your eyes the strength that lies so deep inside of you
We've shared amazing moments along the way
You're blazing a trail
Love will never fail

Reaching for the Reins
Facing those winds of Change
With every hoof beat of your heart
Heels down we're riding on solid ground
We'll say good-bye but never part
From hauling to stalling
To painting white fences
From Lightning to Josie
We will never forget this
Reaching for the Reins
Facing those winds of Change
With every hoof beat of your heart
Heels down we're riding on solid ground
We'll say good-bye but never part

So the next time you're afraid
Just remember your courage …
Reaching for the Reins
Sit tall in the saddle of life
Hey, I'm teachin' my spirit to fly … to … fly.

Chapter 23

More Than Playing with Ponies

Just as astounding as the misconceptions of who alternative kids are is how resilient they are. Even the smallest efforts of someone wanting to help and teach mean so much to those who have a hunger to learn and matter. This is why from its beginning Reaching for the Reins was about horses, hands-on knowledge, and service.

Two things someone can expect with certainty at a horse farm are: horses and work. The list of chores seems only to compound. There are always stalls to clean, fences to mend, things to paint, and projects to be built. And that's just the basic upkeep. By themselves, these chores don't have much appeal; it's the prospect of working with someone that lends these chores their appeal. This fellowship makes participating in these chores one of the most enjoyable parts of being at the farm.

Cal is always the leader of the work detail, which usually starts by filling the Gator with wood, nails and hammers, and screws and screwdrivers. Cal then heads off toward the designated location with a group of kids in tow.

Cal and the students are fortunate to have several volunteers each week join them in projects around the farm. Gina, Christy, Joan,

Ronda, Aimee, and several others are always ready to roll up their sleeves and learn right along with the students. As they work together, they talk to the students about the task at hand, what is going on in their lives, and future goals and plans. These are the interactions that the students crave most of all.

Being the leader of a group of ten eager workers is a bit of a hectic task, but Cal takes it all in stride. While many people have the drive to be self-sufficient in terms of home repairs and building projects, those skills are often hard to self-teach. This is where Cal comes in. For farm projects, Cal walks the students through each part of the task, demonstrating the tricks of the trade he has mastered in his long career as a builder.

One sunny afternoon, Cal's itinerary involved attaching new brackets to the wooden fence posts in order for a new kind of braided wire to be strung. This particular afternoon was the students' first trip to the farm that year, and the anticipation of what lay in store for them hung heavy in the air. After arriving at the farm, Cal corralled a group of students to assist in the project. On the way to the far end of the pasture, Cal explained to the group that rather than using a tape measure to figure out placement for the brackets, they would instead be using a story stick. While they walked, he explained that the story stick was a long stick that he'd held up next to one of the existing fence posts and marked with the location of each of the brackets. Instead of having to measure each post they could simply use the marks on the "story stick" as a guide. Techniques like these are some of the time-saving methods Cal frequently shares with the group.

When the group reached their destination, Cal started one pair of students pulling off old brackets, another pair marking where the new brackets would go, and showing a few more how to use the screw guns to install the new brackets. The group worked like an assembly line. As the students worked, they began talking and joking with each other and getting to know the volunteers.

The skills needed to work a screw gun are generally taken for granted, as, for most people, it's something they've done once or twice over the course of their lives. In actuality, someone who has never had the opportunity and who's never seen it demonstrated might struggle, despite how we might regard its natural ease. Part of Cal's instruction involves showing the students how to change from a bit to a driver, and he has to remind them to keep pressure on the gun to avoid stripping out the screw. This generally takes a few attempts before students get the hang of it.

It's always interesting to me how students tend to step out of their comfort zone in different ways when they are working with tools. When students understand they can learn to do things themselves, a sense of pride is fostered. They are so eager to try new things. Sometimes it looks as though they might be willing to fight over who gets to do the most work. So often they've been told in their secret corners that they are not capable of doing new things, but the volunteers at the farm work hard to ensure that every experience fosters growth and shows students that their goals are not merely attainable, but are easily within their reach.

As the group made their way around the fence line one post at a time, their investment in and determination to get all they could out of the program was readily apparent. Some groups of students take several weeks to understand what Reaching for the Reins is and that they can grow in many ways from their experiences at the farm. This particular group got it from the outset. From week one they seemed to understand that life skills, horses, and service were all up for grabs.

* * *

At the beginning of our fifth year of Reaching for the Reins, I was approached by someone within the school district who said they had not realized that Reaching for the Reins was more than just playing with ponies. It struck me how over the last five years, even after being featured in several newspaper articles and television news broadcasts, people still did not understand who we were and what we'd set out to accomplish. And the same was true for Cedar Lane, which has been around for more than twenty years. The creation of the alternative school gave immediate rise to the assumption that alternative schools are schools for the "bad kids," that when kids get in trouble in a normal classroom they are forced to endure the humiliation of attending the bad kid school. Many of the students from Cedar Lane are not there because they did anything wrong. That society at large remains ignorant of the plight of those around them is frustrating. Many of our students attend Cedar Lane because difficult, sometimes unconscionable things happened to them, for which they were not yet equipped with effective coping methods. Cedar Lane allows them second chances at success, and Reaching for the Reins is a big part of how we help to foster that success. And we do it with more than ponies.

My Challenge to You

Reaching for the Reins has changed my life. What started as a program to encourage students to give back has grown into so much more. The students, volunteers, and I have all embarked on journeys of growth that have led us down paths to becoming better people. I always want my kids to be better people, both for their own good and for the good of those around them, and I see year after year how Reaching for the Reins helps them start that lifetime quest.

My purpose in writing this book has been to share how amazing my students are and how they have chosen to change the courses of their futures for the better. With these stories I also want to encourage anyone who has a dream or an idea to act upon it. Far too often we meet people who have amazing talents that go unshared because of their doubts or fear of failure. Across this incredibly diverse country there are countless nonprofit and service organizations forced to close their doors each year due to a lack of volunteers and funding. If everyone committed to pitching in within their communities to help each other—maybe a few hours or a week or an occasional weekend—our nation could experience a significant social revival. Imagine the possibilities if everyone worked to improve the quality of life for everyone around them. While this idea is admittedly idealistic, perhaps illogically optimistic, the reward is not at all one-sided. Despite having spent countless hours researching and writing grants, tracking student statistics and planning events, facilitating meetings and petitioning media coverage, I have received a reward tenfold from what I have put into the program. I can tell you that the path is not always easy, but it is without question worth every expended effort.

One of the simplest things to do, one of the more popular options, is nothing. And, unfortunately, this is an easy course, a path of no resistance. Too often people believe they have to be in the right place, whether personally, emotionally, or financially, before they can give back. My belief is that service is an integral part of what puts you in that right place and what helps in aligning us. The students from Cedar Lane embark on this experience with many deficits in all facets of their lives. And yet the simple act of putting one's own needs aside and putting others first transforms them and bestows on them an otherwise absent sense of pride, accomplishment, and motivation that helps heal their broken pasts.

It is my challenge to each of you to walk in the footsteps of these incredible students, to step outside your comfort zones and experience the benefits service can offer you and those around you. Most of my students never dreamed they had much to offer. However, they all took a leap of faith, freely giving of their talents, and their reward was twofold: they developed a passion for helping others, becoming agents of positive change in their communities, and they realized they were capable of accomplishing anything they set their mind to, which has expanded their horizons and encouraged them to reach for their dreams.

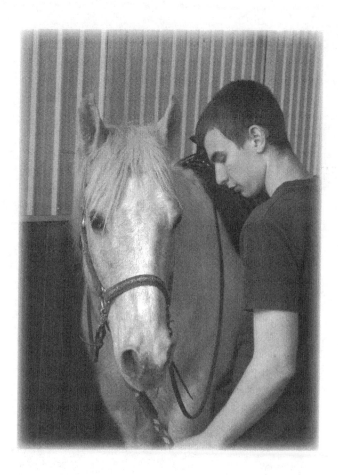

Epilogue

Since compiling and writing this book, I have been blessed to transition from teaching full-time to teaching half-time and running additional service-learning programs for the district. Through developing and facilitating these new programs, I am finding that the service-learning model works for people from all backgrounds and age groups. These other programs have met with many of the same successes.

Shelter Helpers is a program geared for high-school-aged WAY Niles students. The program facilitates student volunteers at the Berrien County Animal Control facility, where they learn to care for and train animals, thereby making them more adoptable. The knowledge and experiences gained from these visits are then incorporated into a project-based learning curriculum.

In the mold of Reaching for the Reins, Stable Paths was created for Niles adult education students. Participants in the program attend Circle "C" Stable, where they learn the teamwork and leadership skills necessary to participate in and run community outreach projects. It also helps them develop connections in the community that may be useful in securing employment after graduation.

Building Futures is a program where Cedar Lane Alternative High School students unite forces with Sarett Nature Center to create projects in the center's woodshop, which are then donated to local organizations and individuals. The knowledge and experiences gained from this are then incorporated into projects geared toward each student's high school graduation requirements.

As I extend the service-learning model to different groups of students and different mediums of service, I have realized several things about the process that I would like to share with you that might enable you to pursue service through your own interests.

1. Pick something about which you are passionate.
   - My passion for horses is obvious to the students and is contagious. It helps that I bring genuine knowledge to the program, and it gives me the drive to stick with all the tedious parts of facilitating the program.
2. Partner with the right people.
   - I am very careful about what organizations I work with. Many organizations are willing to let people volunteer at their facility, but some do not recognize that the students also need to gain from the experience. I look for organizations that are willing to give back as they receive.
3. Have students journal.
   - Writing journals may be the students' least favorite part of the process, but it provides so much insight into what they are thinking, feeling, and gaining from the experience. It is invaluable to me as an educator to see how I can steer the program to help them more. Additionally, I have had countless program alumni tell me that they read through their journals from time to time when they are down and need a pick-me-up or direction in their lives.

4. Track the stats.
    - Statistics make the world go 'round. Grant companies love evidence that your program works, and statistics give you hard-and-fast credibility. I tried tracking several different things before I found data that was meaningful, and I track different things for different programs.
5. Require something of the students.
    - I have found that students need extrinsic motivation to build intrinsic motivation. So I require that they attend school a certain percentage of the time and pass a certain percentage of their classes in order to remain involved in the service-learning programs. After a couple of semesters they usually realize how good success feels, and many continue the pattern of their own accord. Participation in the program is not an entitlement. Holding them accountable for something makes them want to earn it and feel good about earning it.
6. Always have an expert.
    - Even though I am a horse nut, I would not consider myself an expert. For each of my programs I find that I am often tied up in paperwork and facilitation of students, volunteers, and events, and do not have time for planning content. It is extremely important that each program partner with an expert who can teach the students. In most cases it means that I have to provide compensation to the expert, but it is a valuable part of the program that ensures that students are gaining knowledge and experience.
7. Take tons of pictures.
    - Not really an explanation needed here. Students love them, and pictures capture moments that could never be put into words.

8. Develop rock-solid procedures and paperwork.
   - From the first day, you must start with great liability paperwork that covers anything you may want to do with the program. Your paperwork needs to cover safety procedures and policies first and foremost, but also needs to cover publishing and marketing. Having to obtain these after the fact reduces any guarantees on which you may have banked.
9. Learn to write grants and remember to follow up.
   - To date I have received over $100,000 in grant funds. In order to run solid programs it takes funding, and most districts and organizations, unfortunately, do not have budgets for additional programs. However, I have found several generous individuals and grant companies that are willing to support great ideas. Writing grants is not as hard as it seems; you just have to pay attention to all the little details. I have also found it helpful to follow up with grant companies and let them know how programs are going. This makes it easier to ask for money a second time around—they'll remember you when you engage them without any expectation.
10. Say thank you.
    - I try every chance I can to encourage my students to say thank you and to say thank you myself to all the organizations, grant companies, and volunteers who make programs possible.
11. Spread the word.
    - I initially sat on my ideas for five years before I started sharing the accomplishments of Reaching for the Reins and the other service-learning programs I run. I am not a person who enjoys the limelight, so I kept to myself. However, I found that it is very important to

the students to showcase their accomplishments and that because the service model works, it is important to inspire others. So I encourage you from day one to share what you are doing. Share your success and your lessons learned so that you can encourage others to take up the cause.

Each and every year our goal for all the service-learning programs is to make them better. We didn't start off year one with all the answers or programs that were perfect. All of the programs are a continual work in progress. We all try to do our best to keep an open mind and follow the philosophy that we will do whatever is best for kids. Even when the programs were not perfect, we saw huge returns in terms of growth from the students, so there really is nothing to lose in getting started.

For continually updated information about Reaching for the Reins and additional service-learning programs, programs, visit www.reachingforthereins.org.

About the Author

Tara Carlsen is a mathematics teacher for at-risk teens and the creator of the Reaching for the Reins program. She was born and raised in rural southwest Michigan and has always loved horses and the peace that they exude. Early on in her career, she realized her students were not reaching their full potential, and she developed Reaching for the Reins, an equine service-learning program, to teach them teamwork and leadership, and to build students' self-esteem. The program has fostered growth in numerous ways over the past six years for more than 120 students. She lives in southwest Michigan with her husband, two dogs, and horse.

58583730R10137

Made in the USA
Lexington, KY
13 December 2016